D1509556

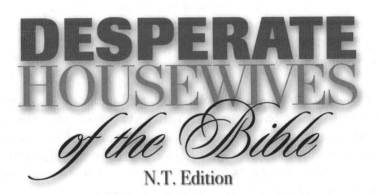

N.T. Edition

Robert Strand

P R E S S

Mobile, AL

Desperate Housewives of the Bible, N.T. Edition
by Robert Strand
Copyright © 2007 Robert Strand

ISBN 978-1-58169-246-4
For Worldwide Distribution
Printed in the U.S.A.

Evergreen Press
P.O. Box 191540 • Mobile, AL 36619

Table of Contents

Other Evergreen Press
books by Robert Strand

Angel at My Door
Desperate Housewives of the Bible, O.T. Edition
The B Word
The Power of Forgiving
The Power of Thanksgiving
The Power of Gift Giving
The Power of Grandparenting
The Power of Motherhood
The Power of Fatherhood
The Power of Debt-Free Living

DEDICATION

To the many women who have been members of the
congregations it has been my privilege to have pastored!
Ladies...thanks for all your patience shown to me,
a man who has attempted to be your minister
in all kinds of situations.
You have provided great insight
into the minds of female thinking and living.
I do not claim to be an expert
but am still a learner.
Thanks for all the life lessons.

And...to all of you readers
who are curious enough
to select and read this book.
Without you, no books would be written.

INTRODUCTION

This volume of *Desperate Housewives of the Bible* is for women and men, clergy or lay-persons, young or old, who are searching for fresh ways of looking at some of the key people of the New Testament. Everybody has a story! Some stories are happy, some are sad, and some are even shocking or depressing. Some are more interesting and should be shared...some are not to be shared.

Stories have a way of shaping our living. I've said it many times, "If your life will be changed for the better in the next five years, likely it will depend on the books you read and the people you meet." As we read a story of someone who has overcome difficulties, we can make an easy application to our own living. Stories have a way of challenging us to help us overcome our preconceived notions and to change. Stories are powerful! Words have meaning and words have life...especially when relating powerful, life-changing principles.

In telling and re-telling the stories of these ladies from the Bible, I have chosen as my method a modified Jewish form of storytelling called *midrash* (the plural form in the Hebrew is *midrashim*). The meaning is "to go in search of" or "to inquire." Midrash is the result of ancient and modern day rabbis going in search of the true meaning of the Scriptures and their applications to living. Most of the midrashim we have record of today originated from sermons preached in synagogues. It's a method of filling in the gaps. Biblical stories can be brief or almost non-existent, especially when dealing with women. I have presented these ladies as telling their own story—a narrative in the first person.

Many biblical women are nameless or their portraits are sketchy at best. For example, take misunderstood and much maligned Mrs. Lot. Her story is written in a short single verse,

"But Lot's wife, behind him, looked back, and she became a pillar of salt" (Genesis 19:26). How do you build her story? You read the context, background, and setting, and extrapolate the kind of a person she might have been, using imagination to fill in the gaps.

This volume is about New Testament women who have interesting stories of shattered dreams, betrayals, rejections, unfulfilled needs, wonderful ministries...and on and on we could go. Desperate? Yes! Finding answers that will work in today's world? Yes! But, perhaps most importantly, these are women with whom God is not finished, and that's where we come into the picture. Use your imagination as you read. See yourself in their situation, and most importantly, discover how answers to their situations might also be the answers you need.

Hopefully you will find this book informative and inspirational. My prayer is that you, the reader, female or male, will be moved, compelled, and even motivated to explore your own lifestyle and stories. I also confess that the writing of these two volumes has been a stretching experience for me. I have been challenged to take another look at myself.

There's one more thing you should know. Secretly, I've always wanted a sister! I grew up with two brothers and only four girl cousins. I have observed how my own daughter relates to her brothers. At times they (daughters) can be the most loveable, wonderful and thoughtful people in the world. At other times, I've been told by their brothers that sisters can make you miserable because they have this habit of telling you what to do and not to do. Some sisters make bad choices, and all you can do is watch them mess up because they refuse your good intentions. Well, all in all, I really do have sisters...biblical sisters. These sisters are just like some of your biological ones. Some have learned life lessons the hard way so that you and I can be spared some of their pain. In writing this book, I have discovered sisters like I have always wanted. And I have discovered these sisters are like sisters of today with some of the same battles we are fighting today.

So join the club...read on, here are some gals who can lift your spirits, encourage you, and teach you lots of life lessons. I hope not to be preachy, but sisters have a way of nagging. After all, did you expect anything else from a sister?

Robert J. Strand
Springfield, Missouri
2007

Chapter One

ANNA

Desperate for redemption!

Anna, as far as can be ascertained, became the first woman to be a Christian missionary! Her name means "favor" or "grace." It's the Phoenician name used by the writer Virgil for the sister of Dido, queen of Carthage. The Old Testament version of Anna is Hannah. The name "Anna" according to Elsdon C. Smith and his book, *The Story of Our Names,* says there are likely more than a million girls and women in America who have this name.

We really know very little of this wonderful widow. Her father was Phanuel, meaning, "the face or appearance of God." I think we can infer that he, too, must have been a devoted person to the things of God. The name of her husband, who died at a premature age, is not given. Her father and family were of the tribe of Asher, one of the so-called "lost tribes of Israel." Her biography is written by the beloved physician, Luke, in only three very short verses.

Scripture: *Luke 2:36-38*

HER SIDE OF THE STORY...

I'd like to welcome you into my very wonderful world! It's likely that I am one of the most famous of all biblical widows.

1

Eighty-four years is a long time to live alone; but please, don't feel sorry for me, I have lived a full, exciting, and fulfilling life. The crowning event happened at the very end. I'm getting ahead of myself. Please excuse me, I'll start at the beginning.

I was born into one of the most wonderful families of my day. My father, Phanuel, was especially devout. He really lived up to his name, "the face or appearance of God." Dad was the kindest, gentlest, most understanding father that a daughter could ever have. He was a happy, joyful man—deeply loved by his family and neighbors, and highly respected in the city of Jerusalem. He portrayed for me and my siblings everything that our loving heavenly Father must be. He modeled behavior that we all followed. I loved my father, and this love took me to a higher dimension in love for my heavenly Father later in my life. As you have already, no doubt, picked up on, I had a wonderful childhood. Our home was a gathering place—Mom always had coffee and fresh bread for anyone who stopped by and, believe me, lots of them came to enjoy her warm, loving hospitality!

Early in life I most naturally turned to the Torah (the first five books of your Bible) because of the reverence and love my father showed to us in his love of God's Word. And there were also the writings of many other prophets such as Isaiah, Jeremiah, and others, as well, such as David's Psalms.

Outside of our home and synagogue family, there wasn't much to be happy about, living in Jerusalem! It had been more than 400 years since we had a real prophet in residence or heard a word from heaven. Spiritually, we were in a desert place. It was a bleak time in our nation. Not only that, we had been conquered many times and even forced into slavery. I grew up under the harsh rule of the Roman Empire. How we yearned to be free! We longed for the coming of the promised Messiah. We were ready for deliverance and redemption! It was a constant topic in our house and synagogue. And yet, lots of people seemingly had given up on His coming. But not my father and, definitely not me!

Although life was hard, I had a wonderful childhood and early teen upbringing. We all know that life changes. As time went on, some men started coming by the house; I guess because either they were just curious or wanted to take a look. At what? Me as a possible bride! You need to understand that marriages in my day were arranged by the parents of the groom together with the parents of the bride-to-be. My father and I had an agreement that if I didn't like what I saw in the prospective husband, I shook my head and he turned down the negotiation. Only if I liked what I saw, could negotiations begin.

In my day, I guess, I was seen as a "classic"—a beautiful, Israeli young lady. To be truthful, I thought myself to be just average and no raving beauty, but the number of men who came calling tells me that they must have thought otherwise.

One man's name was Moshe, and he was handsome, well-mannered, hard working, and had a reputation for his great craftsmanship (he'd already learned his carpentry trade and had a reputation for his craftsmanship and honesty), and I was impressed. So the negotiations began. It was always about the dowry. Secretly, I told my father, "Go easy on Moshe so you don't scare him away." My father played it perfectly, and the wedding date was set. I was ecstatic!

You'd be bored with all the details that went into our wedding—it was simple but as elegant as we could pull off on a shoestring. We were so happy as newlyweds and had many plans for the future. Moshe started his own business, and I helped him in the shop. We planned for a family, and life was good.

The first seven years went by quickly. We were so in love.

Our routines of life had a rhythm of their own with the daily chores to be done. On the Sabbath we'd go to the synagogue together, discuss the lesson afterward, and then plan our future.

In the last month of the seventh year, tragedy struck when Moshe was out felling trees for the next construction job. I was standing in the doorway of our home when I saw some members of the crew running rapidly toward me and gesturing wildly! They shouted, "A tree has fallen on Moshe! Help!"

I ran as fast as I could in the direction of the woods while the men gathered some men to help them. One of them pointed in the direction where they had been working, and I saw the fallen tree. The closer I got, the more fear rose in my throat! Then I saw him pinned to the ground by the giant tree, white as a sheet, barely breathing, his life almost gone...my Moshe! I knelt in the dirt beside him and cradled his head and cried for help.

Moshe faintly moved his lips. "I knew you would come...I love yyoouuuu..." That was all, and he was gone! I was in shock!

The work crew came back with more help and managed to move the tree off my husband. They gently carried his limp body to our humble home, and neighbors helped me prepare his body for burial. It was the saddest day of my life. The one I loved dearly was gone, and now I would be alone. The future of widows in my day was not bright. What would I do? My parents were dead. Where would I live? How would I eat? All important questions for which I had no answer.

The funeral was a blur; I can hardly remember. The time of mourning seemed to go on forever. My friends were of some comfort, but largely I faced my bleak future alone except for the time I spent in prayer, meditation, and reading the Word of God. What a comfort.

My meager funds soon ran out, and I couldn't find a job. A couple of marriage offers came my way, but you should have seen these motley characters who wanted to take advantage of a poor widow. I refused them all. But what would I do for the future?

One day, while in the temple worshipping the Lord, a desire welled up in me, "I'd like to give myself in ministry and service for the Lord and His people in His temple!" Then came this thought, "I need to sell my humble house and move into the temple grounds if such a thing could be arranged!" Immediately I sprang to my feet to search out the High Priest. I told him my idea, and he approved and made the arrangements. God is so good! My house sold immediately, and I moved into a tiny, sparse room. It was humble, but it became my home. I made myself available to the priests and Levites and served them and their needs. I lovingly cleaned the temple. I didn't leave the temple very often but devoted my time to worshipping day and night along with fasting and prayer.

The Lord became my all in all. In the course of time, a special ministry of a prophetic gift was given to me. It was a gift God gave me to encourage the discouraged, lift up the fallen, and always give a word about the coming Messiah! For 84 glorious years, this was my life! A life lived in service to the Lord and His people. It was humbling, and it was a very special "God thing."

I knew all the promises about a coming Messiah and just knew I would see it fulfilled in my lifetime. But time was running out. I was about to celebrate my 100th birthday! Yes, you got it right, brothers and sisters, I was going to be 100 years old! It was unheard of in my day. I knew in my spirit that the Lord had sustained me with a long life which would continue until I saw the child, the fulfillment of God's promises!

The day it happened it was the highlight of my life! It

began just like most every other day until I heard Simeon shouting and praising God: "Sovereign Lord, as you have promised, you may now dismiss your servant in peace for my eyes have seen your salvation, which you have prepared in the sight of all people, a light for revelation to the Gentiles and for glory to your people Israel!"

I was stunned!

Then I heard him gently say to the parents: "This child is destined to cause the falling and rising of many in Israel... And a sword will pierce your own soul too."

I ran as fast as I could to where Simeon stood with the little family. (Well, honey, at my age nobody moves very fast.) When I saw the child, I knew beyond any doubt...this was the child! This was the long-awaited Messiah! I cried, I jumped, I shouted, I gave thanks, and I praised the Lord. It was time to celebrate! This was the greatest event in all of human history, and I had lived long enough to be part of it! God Himself had come down to this wretched world in the form of a baby to show His love to us.

I was so excited to become the first woman missionary, sharing the good news of redemption to all of Jerusalem! Imagine, a 100-year-old widow preaching the Gospel in the streets of our city and beyond.

I had wanted to die with my boots on and I did! I was healthy and strong until my last breath. My mission lasted a few months and on the last day of preaching, I came home, fasted what would have been my last supper, had my evening devotions and fell into bed rejoicing in the goodness of the Lord. I fell asleep on my bed and awakened in the most glorious place imaginable!

WISDOM FOR 21ST CENTURY LIVING FROM ANNA...

What a special life I was privileged to live. The writer Luke captured it completely in just a few words: I was an aged prophetess and, as a widow, I stayed in the Temple and served God with fastings and prayers, giving thanks to the Lord, and I spoke about Jesus Christ to all who would listen. I suppose I am one of those rare human beings who has found the reason for her existence in living for the Lord and praising Him.

This lifestyle might be beyond a possibility in your life. Yet the principles remain the same. Serve the Lord with joy and happiness. Study the Word of God. Give yourself to fasting and prayer. Worship Him as often as possible. Encourage others with a positive message and outlook on life. Devote yourself to a meaningful cause. Remember that life is not a sprint—it's a long distance run. And most important of all, remember that the Lord will never leave you nor forsake you no matter what your situation in life.

I believe David captured the essence of Anna's life with these words:

One thing have I asked of the Lord, that I will seek after, that I may dwell in the house of the Lord all the days of my life, to behold the beauty of the Lord, and to inquire in his temple (Psalm 27:4).

Chapter Two

THE NAMELESS ADULTERESS

Desperate to get away

We know absolutely nothing about this woman, other than her alleged adulterous action. She is one of the many nameless women in the Bible who are only known because of their actions, by the spouse they married, or the other company they kept.

However, Jesus, who came to seek and save the lost, never ran from a confrontation, nor did he ever avoid those who had been caught in their sins. Another interesting thing to note is that Jesus never called anyone a "sinner." Oh, yes, he had some descriptive words when describing hypocrites or religious leaders who were not really religious at all. (But that's for another book.)

Scripture: *John 8:1-11*

HER SIDE OF THE STORY...

I shall always be remembered as "that woman who was caught in the act of adultery!" I wasn't always that bad, but my life had taken all kinds of twists and turns. Yes, I did make some very bad life choices. Maybe, just maybe, if you had been in my situation, you might have done what I did. Now I'm not proud of this act nor the poor choices I made. Think of me as an object lesson on what not to do with your life. I've been

8

prattling on and not making much sense. Just remember that I'm not really trying to excuse myself or blame others for the bed I laid in.

Life was okay until my folks arranged a marriage for me with the meanest, nastiest, dirtiest old man you can imagine. He had money, however, and paid a handsome dowry for my hand in marriage. I nearly gagged the first time he touched me—my flesh crawled. I never got used to the way he abused me sexually. I was desperately trapped. I prayed for his untimely death so I could be free. There was absolutely no love between us. I was simply his sex object to be used. But in my situation, and in my day, you couldn't easily get divorced if you were a woman.

I shopped frequently at the same booths in the open market because it was easier that way. I immediately noticed a handsome, young, virile merchant looking at me each time I went by his booth, and he smiled. I stopped to check out his merchandise and engaged in conversation. He was so kind and interested in me—sparks of emotion began flying between us. Here was somebody who cared about me. Need I tell you that I was flattered? One thing led to another and soon, in the middle of the day when my husband was working in the field, this merchant came by. We had a hot and heavy extra-marital affair as you call it—a nice name for adultery.

But it wasn't long until I found out my lover had a wife and family, and he broke our relationship off. It wasn't much longer until I found another lover, and then another, and another. I pretty well kept it from my unsuspecting husband, but somehow the neighbors knew.

Word somehow must have spread among the male members of our community because I had no problem finding all kinds of guys who loved to stop by. One day, a member of the Sanhedrin itself made a pass at me. Now, here was a high-class lover. He was an upper-crust kind of a guy with clean finger-nails and all. He was a community leader, highly respected because of his religious occupation. We had a torrid affair. He loved to catch me still in my bed after my husband had left for the fields. We sure had fun until one early morning...

Just as the sun was beginning its move across the bright blue azure sky, a bunch of the religious "Mafia" came bursting into the room where we were locked in a passionate embrace and shouted, "We caught you!" My lover hopped up, grabbed his clothes, and reached for the bag of silver one of the Pharisees held out to him as he made his way out of my bedroom with a smirk on his face! He didn't even look back.

Two of them jerked me up and out of bed and started out the door with me, not a stitch of clothes. "Please...let me get dressed." As I dressed, I realized I'd been had...it was a set up. *Why me? What have I done to deserve this? Where are they taking me and why? Where is my lover? They just let the jerk go...but they've got me!*

Among the Sanhedrin and Pharisees (who were teachers of the Law), there was much bantering and speculation. At first I thought they were dragging me into the temple courts, but I soon realized that they were taking me in front of the crowd who had gathered to hear the new teacher, the miracle-worker we had heard so much about. I decided that they wanted to make an example of me before him, and in public at that! I was a disheveled mess. Never in all my life was I so humiliated. The crowd smirked, laughed, poked each other and said, "Take a look at her." They all seemed to know what was going to happen...all but me.

They propelled me to the front where Jesus was sitting and teaching the crowd. They made me stand in front of him and before the laughing and hooting crowd. They were sure getting their money's worth this morning. There I stood, shivering in the cool morning, scared out of my wits. What was going to happen now?

They leveled their fingers at the teacher and at me and triumphantly gloated, "Teacher, we caught this woman in the act of adultery!" I thought, *Yeah, okay, it happens a lot in this town. Where are they going with this—these hypocritical law enforcers?*

They shouted, "In the Law, Moses commanded us to stone such a woman!" They knew there hadn't been a woman stoned in the last 400 years, let alone the guilty man. And where was my lover—the law said that both the man and the woman were to be stoned when they were caught in adultery. Where is he? It dawned on me that they must have bribed him into betraying me so he was part of the set-up! Then I began to really be afraid. They were more than capable of throwing stones at me, as worked up as they were! I was getting sick to my stomach.

Then they delivered the punch line: "Now what do you say?" They knew that on the one hand, Jesus said he came to fulfill the Law. On the other hand, he was teaching on loving one another, and stoning a woman really didn't fit in with that teaching. It seemed as though Jesus was trapped with no way out! These so-called custodians of the Law, these self-appointed self-righteous moral inspectors, were at their meanest. They were gloating because the perfect trap had been set and sprung. Their zeal against my sins was a thin covering for their own vileness. I was so mad that I was ready to begin to name the names of all those guys who had also been in my bed.

The most incredible thing happened at this point—the teacher knew it was a trap and simply bent down and started to write with his finger in the dust and dirt on the temple court floor. While he wrote they kept firing questions, but as they began to read what he was writing, they slowed down and began to get quiet.

He pulled himself to his full height, and I saw fire in his eyes as he took in this bunch of accusers. He looked each in the eye until their gaze fell. They couldn't look back. Then he said the most astonishing statement I have ever heard: "You who thinks he is without sin, pick up the first stone and throw it at her." They stood there, stunned, caught in the glare of his question and the on-looking crowd.

You'll never believe what the teacher did next...he bent down and began writing again...this time he wrote names and hidden sins! My head was down so I was reading as he wrote. They were all names everyone recognized. Then I heard quiet shuffling and glanced up. This bunch of hypocrites began to disappear like a snowball on a July day—from the oldest who had the longest list of sins down to the youngest. They slunk away like the guilty rats they were.

After they all had left, Jesus stood up and looked at me for the first time. Never in all my life had anyone looked at me so lovingly like He did—not with a sensual kind of love, but kindly just like he could see all the way through me. I can't explain what was happening inside of me. Then He said, "Lady...where have they all gone? Who is your accuser, now?"

"No one, Lord," I replied. Was I ever relieved. The crowd that had seen what happened was still there on the edge of their seats, straining to catch what He was about to say.

He looked at me and softly said, "Then, neither will I condemn you!" I wanted to shout! He set me free! Wave after wave of relief flowed over me. It was as if I had been carrying a 100 pound pack up the mountainside, and he just lifted it off me. It felt incredible to be free!

I knew he meant business, and I just knew I had to obey. He gave me a new focus, a new way of living when he said gently but firmly, "Go now...you are free...but you must leave your life of sin."

I promised myself that is exactly what I would do. Talk about receiving a second chance, an opportunity to turn my life around! With his help and words ringing in my heart and soul, I knew a new way of living was possible.

WISDOM FOR 21ST CENTURY LIVING FROM THE LIFE OF A NAMELESS, FORGIVEN ADULTRESS...

Somehow I wish we had more of this lady's story. I believe she went away from that encounter with a clean heart and was a forgiven person, free to begin a new way of living.

The lessons are many. We all can be sure that eventually our sins will find us out. Payday isn't always on Friday but, you can bet your bottom dollar that someday, somewhere you will be found out. What do we do then?

I don't know where you might place adultery on the list of the top ten sins—it's bad, but not impossible to be forgiven! We have a Savior, a Friend who is closer than blood relatives who is willing to forgive us.

No matter how diabolical or evil or vile you may be or have been, you too can be forgiven when the Master of life comes into your life.

Forgiveness is not enough; repentance calls for a turning around, a whole new way of living. The miracle of the moment is that we are forgiven, but it needs to be followed up with a life lived in such a way as to please God.

If you need forgiveness, if you need to be set free from your past, no matter how sordid, there is hope for you. There is salvation for you and most of all there is divine forgiveness! All of this is found in a relationship with the Creator of the universe and his one and only Son!

Chapter Three

SALOME #1

A desperate dance of death!

 Salome is the female form of the name of Solomon in the Hebrew language. However, the Greek form means *shalom* or "peace." Another scholar tells us that the name Salome really implies, "very shady" which may be a better indicator of the debased character of the daughter of Herodias.

The Bible does not name her other than referring to her mother. It is the noted Jewish scholar, Josephus, who identifies this daughter as Salome. She was the daughter of Herodias by her first husband, Herod Philip, a son of Herod the Great.

Salome later first married Philip the tetrarch, and later Aristobulus, king of Chalcis, the grandson of Herod and brother of Agrippa. Quite a family for Salome.

Scripture: *Matthew 14:6-11; Mark 6:14-29*

HER SIDE OF THE STORY...

What can I say to change your already made-up mind about me? You, no doubt, like all the others, have pictured me as a low-life—morally bankrupt. You know what? I really don't care! I loved my reputation and did everything I could to live up to it no matter what. Life in a palace isn't always a cake-walk, you know.

Likely you don't think much better of my family and extended family, either. You're right again. We were the ruling class—ruthless, incestuous, and abusive. But you have to admit that we did know how to hold onto power. So, can you blame me for the way I turned out? I was a proud product of a sensual lifestyle that I learned from some of the best. Maybe our way of life wasn't too different from some of your ruling class in your world. So what has changed? People are still the same no matter in what time they happen to live. The human psyche hasn't changed in thousands of years. People are still people! (Sorry, I guess I've gotten off track.)

The only interest you may have in me is what happened to an honest, truth-speaking, prophet of God who opened his mouth when he should have kept it closed. You can't mess with my Grandpa and get away with it. And you can't mess with my mother and live to tell about it.

Roman history tells you that I was the product of a broken home, caught in the middle of Mom and Dad and Grandpa and my uncle, who became my stepfather. How's that for a mess?

My mom was a social climber who didn't quit until she was at the top. It was her second marriage to her husband's brother that gave her a final place at the top rung of life. And of course, she brought me along.

To be frank, the palace insulates you from most of the human struggle. Sometimes we're the last ones to know what goes on in the real world. Along with the other palace kids, I only heard bits and pieces of scary stories. For example, my step-grandpa once had all the innocent little boys slaughtered so he could get rid of a poor Jewish family's boy child. It was a story about some astronomers, a star, and some gifts.

On their way to Bethlehem, they stopped at the palace because they were lost and needed directions to find the new king. Grandpa Herod told them the way to go and that when they found the newborn king, they should return and tell him so he could worship the little one, too. What a farce! He only wanted to kill the baby. Why? Ruling kings can't allow any rivals. This had all happened about 30 years earlier, long before my time. I couldn't sleep for nights after hearing the story.

My step-dad, Herod, seemed to be a nicer guy, but I soon discovered he had a hair-trigger temper. A guy named John who dressed in weird clothes and ate grasshoppers and honey, had looked my step-dad in the eye and told him he was doing wrong by marrying my mother, the wife of his brother. John didn't back down—he was fearless. He told my dad he would go straight to hell because of his sin! You don't say such things to a Herod, so John landed in one of step-dad's nasty dungeons. But I must say, my step-dad was also afraid of this man because he was a popular preacher. Herod didn't dare touch John, but he was also fascinated by him and loved to listen to him preach. It was a love-hate relationship on my step-dad's part, I think.

But not my mom! She went absolutely ballistic! She vowed to get even with him even if it was the last thing on earth she did! I mean, there is hatred, and then there's my mom! Talk about holding a grudge. She shook her finger in John's face and spewed out her venom. I've never seen anything like this in my life! She was always after my step-dad to do something about this prophet to shut him up forever!

All kinds of activities were brewing around the palace the year I turned sixteen. The nation was all set to celebrate my step-dad's birthday. It was to be the biggest bash of the year. Everybody who was anybody was personally invited—the ruling class, who were wealthy, snooty, powerful politicians, and socialites. Your Mark Twain described us as a "bunch of crumbs held together by dough."

I knew all of this meant a real dress-up occasion for me. Mom made sure all my physical attributes would be shown off to their greatest advantage. I had a gorgeous, designer gown— filmy, gauzy, and sensual. I knew I'd be stunning in it. What a night this promised to be. I could hardly wait.

Of course, my step-dad and mom were the center of attention. It was Herod's night to shine, and it was obvious he was drunk and filled with his own self-importance as were most of the guests! I was even allowed to drink that night.

The party was moving into high-gear, and the crowd wanted more and more entertainment. Count on my mother to take things up a notch. She motioned for me and whispered, "Honey, here's your opportunity to strut your stuff. How about a dance for dear old dad? (Dancing in my day was a single-sex activity...no couple dances like you might do. And, the more sensual, the better.)

That night was the best! I performed the dance as a birthday present for my step-dad, whom I dearly loved. I looked deeply into his eyes and poured it on. I could tell he loved it! The crowd went crazy, especially when I threw a couple of scarves into the crowd. It became a frenzy, and I was leading it wildly.

If I must say so myself, it was an "Oscar-winning" performance! I was breathless and lathered in sweat and not much clothing. Step-dad motioned me closer and, in front of this crowd, he loudly promised me anything I wanted, up to half of his kingdom, even if he had to take out a mortgage. Heady stuff for a 16-year-old! I didn't know what to ask for, but I knew Mom would help me.

For Mom this was like the coming together of the perfect storm! She already had a plan in place. "Ask your dad for the head of John the Baptist on a platter! And have it done right now!"

Really, the head of a man? Ugh! Gross! This is my once-in-a-lifetime opportunity, and Mom wants me to ask for this guy's head? I couldn't believe it.

I looked at her again. She reassured me, "Yes, my dear, you heard me right. The head of John the Baptist. Now! Don't worry, I'll make it up to you. You'll see."

I hurried back to center stage with this sadistic demand, "I want you to give me—right now—the head of John the Baptist on a platter!"

You should have seen the look on my step-dad's face! He knew it wasn't my idea but my mom's. But he was trapped, with no good way out. He had made a rash promise in front of his guests, and he was really distressed. His pride and his kingdom were on the line. No one wanted a weak, wimpish king. He had no choice!

The major head-chopper was summoned and sent to prison with orders. The crowd was all abuzz. In just a few short minutes, the executioner appeared. Sure enough, the silver platter held the bloody head of John the Baptist. Blood was overflowing the platter and spattering on the floor. Some of the guests took a look and fainted dead away. It was the goriest thing I had ever seen. His eyes were wide open, frozen with surprise. I almost gagged. I was ready to up-chuck when the man brought the bloody mess to me. I grabbed it and ran to my mother and set in her lap as she smiled with victory! I ran for the door and lost my supper in the hallway.

Mom reveled in her revenge. Me, I suffered nightmares month after month! I couldn't lose the sight of that bodiless head staring back at me.

There you have it—my claim to fame. I shall be forever linked with the untimely death of one of your God's servants. There's really nothing more for me to say—I was a guilty accomplice of my mother's. I have often wondered what would have happened if I had refused to do what she had asked. That would not have been a pretty sight, but at least I might have spared the life of a truth-telling servant of your God. I never did ask forgiveness or repent for this deed. I saw no point to it so I went to my grave defiant in the actions I had taken.

WISDOM FOR 21ST CENTURY LIVING
FROM THE LIFE OF SALOME #1...

Some of you may be thinking, "We can't really blame a 16-year-old for her actions." Why not? Although you can't choose your parents, how you are nurtured, or your environment, there comes a time in your life when you must take responsibility for your own actions. Shouldn't it have been a time for her to make a choice rather than go along with mommy dear?

John the Baptist was the fore-runner of Jesus Christ and considered by many in his day as the greatest prophet who ever lived. He confronted evil where he found it, no matter the cost. What would happen if all of us were willing to pay the price and speak the truth?

Chapter Four

SALOME #2

Desperate for her son's success

Please don't mix this Salome with the other Salome, even though they happened to be contemporaries in their day. For the meaning of her name, refer to Salome #1. Legends have sprung up attempting to connect Salome to Joseph through a previous marriage or making her the daughter of Zacharias or presenting her as a sister of Mary, the mother of Jesus. The Bible is silent as to her genealogy, however.

We do know she was the wife of Zebedee, a fisherman prosperous enough to have hired help. We meet him at his boat, mending his nets, when Jesus came by and invited his two sons, James and John, to follow him. We can infer that Zebedee must have shared his wife's devotion to Jesus since he did not try to prevent his sons or his wife from following Jesus. It speaks to us of quite a devoted family, a family in harmony and agreement.

Scripture: *Matthew 4:21; 20:20-24; 27:56; Mark 1:19-20; 10:35-40; 15:40-41; 16:1-2*

HER SIDE OF THE STORY...

I'm not exactly sure where to begin because there is so much I'd like to share. My parental home was a great place to grow into maturity with loving, understanding parents. They were great role models for the home we established when I married Zebedee, who was one great husband and father. We had two boys and did our best to raise them to be God-fearing, hard-working young men. They worked as partners with their father in our little wholesale fish business. Life was wonderful until one day when it all changed.

We had heard of the birth of a promised Messiah. And there was rumor of his having appeared at the age of 12 in the synagogue where even the teachers were astonished at his knowledge and teachings. He had dropped out of sight until the days of the preaching of John the Baptist. One day he appeared on the banks of the river and asked to be baptized. The most amazing thing happened—as Jesus came up out of the water, the heavens burst open and the crowd (our little family was present that day) saw the Spirit of God come out of the sky in the form of a dove and land on his right shoulder! We all sensed something very special was happening, like history in the making.

The next thing is beyond my ability to describe it. As I experienced it, the most awesome, powerful voice I've ever heard spoke so all of us could hear, "This is my Son! I love him! I am well pleased with him! Listen to him!" It was the most unbelievable event I had ever witnessed. I felt surely that this man was the promised Messiah, and I had a ring-side seat!

Then, suddenly, Jesus was led away and seemingly disappeared. We found out later that he had gone into the desert for 40 days of fasting. It was a time of preparation before he began his ministry. This event made the major news for the next 40 days! It was the talk of all of us present at his Baptism. The excitement could be cut with a knife. We weren't sure what was going to happen next.

When Jesus came out of the wilderness, there was something different about him—perhaps a special anointing. He settled in Capernaum and began his preaching ministry. The crowds were awesome, and our family attended many of his meetings. I had never before heard anybody preach like he did, so different from our rabbis. Jesus preached with power and authority and was fascinating to listen to. He promised the kingdom of heaven would quickly be coming to Israel.

One day as Jesus was walking along the Sea of Galilee, he invited (maybe more like commanded) Peter and his brother Andrew to follow him, and he would make them "fishers of men!" What an awesome concept! You bet, they obeyed.

He kept on walking (now there were three), and Jesus spotted my two boys, James and John, in our company boat with their father Zebedee, and he called them to follow him too. My boys didn't hesitate! They left Dad and the boat and everything else and followed him. Now there were five young men. He called eight more young Jewish boys to follow him until there were 13 in all. They were all fine young men—what a happy group! You should have seen them smiling, talking, laughing, arguing, shouting, enjoying each other, and most of all, feeling privileged to be with Jesus.

Well, mother that I am, my first thought was, *Who is going to take care of these young men? Who is going to feed them? Who is going to wash their clothes? Who is going to mother them? Who is going to help them find shelter each night?* The thought struck me like a dagger—me, a mother who knows how to cook and bake and clean up and wash clothes and all the other things a mother will do. I knew they couldn't be traveling evangelists without my help and the help of other women! Need I tell you that behind every successful man there is successful mother doing the cleaning. I wasn't called; I just enlisted along with other volunteers. What a troop we made—going from town to town was really exciting, but hard work for us women.

We witnessed miracles, provisions, healings, and always spectacular preaching. I was privileged beyond my expectations to be an intricate part of the inner workings of this ministry. I didn't have time to keep a diary, I was so busy. But you can read of our life and times in the four Gospel accounts that were written. In fact, I'm so proud that my son John wrote an epistle plus other books in the Bible. (I'd recommend you read it for yourself.)

Would you allow me to tell you something about Jesus, from a woman's eyewitness point of view? Many of your theologians, songwriters, preachers, and artists have all missed the essence of Jesus. They have pictured him as being somber, solemn, aloof, and focused. Have you seen any pictures of him smiling, joyful, and happy. No! And that's too bad! You should have seen him in action. He was an outdoorsman and walked everywhere he went. And because of his work as a carpenter, he was in great shape—a man in the prime of life.

You should have seen the children flock to him everywhere he went. You know, kids are not attracted to sad sacks! Women adored him and followed him. Men respected him and trusted his wisdom and teachings.

I vividly remember the day he went into the Temple and overturned the tables of the money changers and the merchants. Nobody dared challenge him! He raised a heavily muscled arm and overturned the merchants' tables; not even the Temple guards dared to attempt to stop him. He didn't stop until he had cleaned out the entire area! Yet, he was also gentle—not in a feminine way, but out of strength that was under control. I'm really sorry the people of your day have created a wrong picture of Him.

Oh, how I loved him and what he was doing for our suffering and hurting people. He gave them not only hope and help but also health. Above all, he gave us an entirely new concept of who God the Father really is. It was glorious. Words can't paint the real picture.

If you have never really met this man Jesus, I invite you to stop a moment and pray a simple prayer to invite him to be your Savior and your Lord! My son John captured it all with the most memorized Bible verse of your day, "For God so loved the world that he gave his one and only Son, that whoever believes in him shall not perish but have eternal life." What about you? Are you a follower of his? If you aren't, this is my personal invitation for you to become one.

Let me get back on track. Well, our wonderful experience traveling with Jesus lasted a bit more than three years. In the last few months we saw a change in direction. Jesus seemed to be more focused; his teachings were more pointed. There were subtle changes in his attitude, as though he were preparing for his own death. We were saddened. Along with some others, I was sure that he would set up an earthly kingdom and overthrow the hated Roman Empire.

Being the good Jewish mother that I am, I wanted the very best for my James and John. So one day I brought them to Jesus and boldly made a request, "Master, when you establish your kingdom and sit on your throne, would it be possible for James to sit on one side and John on the other so that they could be your next-in-command?"

His answer was a surprise; it was only later that I realized how prophetic it would be. "Can you drink the cup I will be drinking out of?" he pointedly asked James and John. Looking back I can see that he meant, "Will you be willing to die the death I will die?"

Bless their hearts, both answered together, "We can!"

Jesus gently went on, "Yes, you will see me die, and you will die for my sake. However, it's not my place to decide who sits where."

You can imagine what happened when the other ten overheard this conversation! They immediately became angry with my guys and, I guess, with me, too. But Jesus turned it into another teaching principle and told us and the whole world that the way to the top is reserved for those who serve the best.

It was just a few short days later that Jesus was crucified. It was the most excruciating pain I've ever experienced when we saw him beaten and hung on a cross. All of us women watched it from a distance. When it was over, Joseph took the body and laid it in his personal tomb since none of us had time for preparation of the body because of the Sabbath.

When the Sabbath was over, the two other Marys and I bought spices to anoint his body and sadly made our way to the tomb. We asked each other the question, "Who can roll away the stone from the entrance to the tomb?"

When we arrived, we found that the large stone was already rolled away! Cautiously we made our way inside and found a young man in a white robe, and we were afraid!

With a huge smile he said, "Don't be alarmed. Jesus is not here. He has risen from the dead!" The news absolutely stunned us! He was alive!

The young man continued, "Look for yourself. But go and tell the others, and you will be able to see him soon in Galilee! Do you remember that this is what he promised you?"

We ran; we trembled; we were bewildered; we didn't tell anybody else because we were afraid. But not Mary Magdalene—she ran to tell the disciples. Unfortunately they didn't believe her!

But one of my boys believed, and Peter and John ran back to check for themselves. John outran Peter because he was younger and faster, but he didn't go into the tomb. Finally the truth hit all of us, exploded in our minds and we believed—

Jesus is alive! Jesus is no longer dead! What happy news! The greatest news in all of human history!

That's really the end of my story. I was privileged to see my two sons play an important role in the building of a new organization called, "The Church." James became the pastor of the first church in Jerusalem and later one of the first to die for his faith.

John became the "Revelator" and was the last of the original twelve to pass away at the age of ninety-six. What a legacy my boys left on this world, and it was my joy to have been a part of it all.

WISDOM FOR 21ST CENTURY LIVING FROM THE LIFE OF SALOME...

There are many life principles to be taken from this lady and her story. Let's make an attempt to capture some of these.

There is nothing else to compare to a loving family to instill into the life of kids powerful principles with which to live a purposeful life. Zebedee and Salome seemed to be on on the right track when it came to raising their boys.

A true believer in the person and principles of Jesus Christ will also become a devoted follower. In the bottom line of life, what are you really living for? What is your purpose? Where will you find your focus?

Apparently when Salome saw a need, she was willing to fill it. She became part of the company who worked behind the scenes to allow the ministry of Jesus to reach his world.

She also had ambition and desired the best for her family. Ambition is commendable when it's in agreement with the purposes of God.

Chapter Five

THE POOR WIDOW

A desperate offering

 Of all the nameless women of the Bible, this is one sacrificial widow all of us would love to know more about. We only are told about her offering in the Temple one day. That's it. We are grateful for the notice Jesus gave her and the praise he heaped on her because of her sacrifice. She has left an example for all of us in the matter of devotion.

The situation of a widow in her day was a precarious existence. Deprived of a husband and protector, she would have been exposed to all kinds of nasty actions and extortions. If she had grown children, her existence would have been somewhat better. She would always stand out in a crowd because of the distinctive garb she was forced to wear. Thankfully the early church cared for these widows who had no social net and meted out punishment for people who treated widows with disdain. Still, it was not a desirable situation for a woman to have to live under.

Scripture: *Mark 12:41-44; Luke 21:1-4*

HER SIDE OF THE STORY...

Right up front...I'll have you know that really I am just a simple woman raised in a simple home for one purpose in life:

to get married and raise a family. Because my circumstances were humble, my parents were unable to raise much of a dowry, so I married a simple man.

During our married life we always struggled to have enough to eat, wore plain but comfortable clothes, and lived in a tiny house with not much money left over for luxuries. The highlight of our simple lifestyle was to be able to go to the Temple for worship each Sabbath. My husband and I found it to be an uplifting experience to mingle with the crowds and join in the worship. We brought such offerings as we could. I became devoted to the Lord and his worship. It was a relationship I lived for.

All of this changed when my husband died after a lingering disease. During the last few weeks of his life, we used up everything we had saved and put aside for our future. It was exhausting taking care of him and working enough to put some food on the table. Then he died, and my status became that of widow. It was as though I entered a whole new world as an outcast. The widows in our day were immediately relegated to a second-class status. I worked my fingers to the bone just to exist. Yet the highlight of my life still was going to the Temple and worshiping the Lord.

At the end of one particular week, I had only managed to earn two mites, which equaled a single farthing. (A "mite" was the smallest copper coin of the reign of Herod Antipas. Two mites equaled a "farthing" which was the next smallest copper coin, less than a penny in your day.) I had nothing for food for the next week.

I clutched these two mites in my fingers. I decided they would be my offering and the next week I would lean on God to provide for me. You know, he never let me down. I had learned that when I put God first, he would take care of me like he took care of the lilies and the sparrows.

During the celebration of worship that day, it soon was time for the offering. I watched as the wealthy cast in their gold coins, making a loud noise when they dropped them into the chests. Most of them made sure others saw their large, generous sums. How I wished I was able to give like them. Then came the scribes and other religious leaders with their proud display of gifts. Then the crowd thinned and us poor folks made our way forward. I gently dropped in my two copper coins and there was barely a tiny tinkle. My offering was so small I didn't think anybody even noticed.

Then I went on home to begin another week. But something happened inside of me when I gave everything I had. I cannot explain it. I guess it was the joy of giving. I felt as though I was walking on air as I made my way home.

WISDOM FOR 21ST CENTURY LIVING
FROM A POOR WIDOW...

I don't believe this widow ever knew she had been watched by the Son of the living God as she gave sacrificially. Without a doubt, she gave the most spectacular offering ever, according to Jesus. What a legacy for all time!

Even though this widow was poor in earthly goods, she was rich in her devotion to the Lord and his Temple on earth. Jesus measured her giving and the giving of others not by the amount they had given but by what was in their hearts when they gave it.

Jesus is interested in the smallest of gifts and the most humble of people and their circumstances. Little things are important in the kingdom of heaven. In our materialistic world we tend to look down on anything that is little, but not God!

Take heart...even the hairs on your head are numbered and He sees the littlest sparrow fall. Don't give up! The Lord is watching, even today, and takes notice of the smallest sacrifice of your life.

Chapter Six

THE WOMAN AT THE WELL

Desperate for a real drink

 The shortest distance between two points is a straight line, unless you were a Jew in biblical times. The shortest distance from Jerusalem to Galilee was through Samaria, but the Jews, led by the Pharisees, always took the longer route through Peraea. Why? The Jews hated the Samaritans. This hostility can be traced back to the Assyrian colonization of Israel, followed by the antagonism of the Samaritans to the Jews at the return from captivity. This led to the building of rival temples on Mt. Gerizim. There was an unbelievable religious hatred between these two closely related peoples.

The Jews used to say, "He who eats the bread of a Samaritan is as he who eats swine's flesh." The Jews had no dealings with the Samaritans, but Jesus did! He was and is above all religious prejudices and taught us to worship God in spirit and in truth.

Scripture: *John 4:2-42*

HER SIDE OF THIS STORY...

Let's get something straight right up front—I am a Samaritan and proud of it! Why is this important? Because the Jews and Samaritans were feuding for years and years. We loved to call each other insulting kinds of names. We avoided each other; we didn't even talk to each other; if given the chance, we spat on each other. It's just like your Hatfields and McCoy's—only we didn't have shotguns.

Besides being a Samaritan, I was also considered a slut by my own people. Yes, I had five husbands and now I live with a man who is not my husband. You may be thinking, "How could any woman survive five husbands?" Well, in my day, husbands didn't last long, what with warfare, famine, disease, bugs, pestilence, poor health, unsanitary conditions, back-breaking labor, and fatal injuries—men didn't live long. And widows in our society were doomed to become destitute or worse, so it was incumbent that we widows must keep on marrying. My first husband was a winner, but the rest...ah, well, to be nice about it, things sort of went downhill from there. Husband #2 was a physical abuser, #3 was a drunken sot, #4 was a compulsive gambler, and #5 was a complete loser no matter how you looked at things. I tried to keep myself up so I could be ready to catch another, but to marry a sixth man, I just couldn't stand the thought, so we just lived together like so many folks are doing in your day. Not a good thing to do, I must admit. Enough of my boring background. I must get on with the real story of my life.

That day when I came to fill my water pots (it was always us women who went to the well every day), I noticed this man sitting by Jacob's well. Upon getting up close, I realized he was a Jew! What in the world was he doing in Samaria? I figured that he must have gotten lost. It was a blazing hot day and I thought he must be thirsty. What was I to do? He was empty handed, so how was he to get a drink? I was the only woman there at the time because I didn't want to put up with the gossips at their regular time of day to get water when it was cooler. It was midday and hot!

He broke the silence by saying, "Will you give me a drink?" He was polite, sensitive to my feelings, and did not insult me like some of the others regularly did.

A Samaritan woman was on the bottom rung on the Jewish scale. Imagine him asking me for something! But I'm not exactly a shy wallflower. I'm usually brash and a bit forward. (After all, how could I catch six different men by being shy?) So I blurted out, "You're a Jew and I'm a Samaritan woman. How is it that you would dare ask me for a drink?"

He didn't answer my question. He just said something surprising about a different kind of water. "Living water" he called it.

Confused, I asked him, "Where are you going to get this living water? You don't even have a bucket." As if he didn't already know his situation. But that didn't stop me, I just plowed on ahead, "Are you greater than Jacob?" What nerve I had!

Then this man said something really startling, "Whoever [meaning me, too] drinks of my kind of water will never get thirsty again!"

Unbelievable! I had never heard of anything like this. It was almost too good to be true. I wanted this kind of water! I quickly replied, "Sir, give me this water and I will never have to come back to this well again."

"Go get your husband and come back!" Couldn't he have asked me something easier?

I decided to tell him the sordid truth, "I don't have a husband."

"Right," he said, "you have had five of them and the one you currently live with is not a husband. You told me the truth." This was really scary. This man, whoever he was, had read my mail.

Then I made one of those unbelievable, humorous, dumb,

one-liners for all of recorded history, "Sir, I can see you are a prophet." Anything to divert attention away from my situation. Okay, so I stuck my foot into my mouth all the way to my ankles. What next? I kept on plowing ahead with a theological type of question, which is always good to keep things going. I really thought I was clever. "Our fathers..." "You Jews..." "Worship..." "Jerusalem..."—these were words I used that were all hot buttons in my day. My smoke screen didn't throw him off track.

He replied, "Believe me, woman, Jehovah is your salvation." That I understood.

He went on, "True worshippers will worship in spirit and in truth because these are the kind of worshippers the heavenly Father is seeking after." This was a new concept for me, but I was still confused.

I thought, *Enough of this Jewish stuff, I'll get him off track and at the same time show off my knowledge.* "I know that the Messiah is coming, and when he gets here he will explain everything!" I said.

I figured that should shut him up. But what he said next was absolutely unbelievable. And the fact that he said it to me, a Samaritan woman and a fornicator too was amazing. I think he knew that I was one thirsty woman for bottom-line truth.

He looked at me with the most compassionate look I had ever experienced, with his eyes piercing all the way through me, and gently said, "I am that Messiah!"

It was more truth than I could stand. Imagine, he revealed himself to me—a nobody. The Messiah! The Christ! I didn't know what to say, I was speechless for the longest time. Me, who was always ready with a quick comeback.

At this very moment, His disciples appeared and didn't say a word but just took in the whole scene. I can only imagine what they were thinking. I believed Him! I believed Him! The truth of it flashed through my entire being. I felt something I had never felt before. In a moment I was finally able to lay down my burdens and get set free from my self-made prison. It's beyond explanation. His words were like the most refreshing drink of water I had ever had. I forgot all about my water pot because I had found the real fountain of water.

My first thought was, *I've got to tell somebody! In fact, I'll tell the whole town!* And with this in mind, I ran back to town. I didn't care; I began shouting with joy, "He told me everything! Come and see this man! He is the Messiah...really! Come and see for yourself!" Many of them believed me and followed me back to the well. I was bursting with joy and excitement!

I don't know about you, but when I met this Christ, something happened inside of me. I openly confessed my sins! I wanted to share this good news of forgiveness with everyone I knew and even with those I didn't know.

Why did the people of my humble town believe me? I think it was because they could see a dramatic change in me; it was Jesus Christ that made me a new creature!

Jesus stayed with us, outcast Samaritans that we were, for two whole days and we had a revival. I was accepted into the community because of my witness and my changed life. All my neighbors wanted what I had found. What a glorious two days it was. Come to think of it, I suppose I must have been the very first missionary for the Messiah.

The people in my own town came to the same conclusion that I had, "This man is really the Savior of the world!"

I should also tell you that when I finally got home that first night, I had a long talk with my Jake. "It's time you made me an honest woman...let's get married right away." Surprisingly he agreed with me. And we went to the Messiah, and he tied the knot and gave us his blessing!

WISDOM FOR 21ST CENTURY LIVING
FROM THE LIFE OF A THIRSTY WOMAN...

The lessons learned from this fascinating encounter are many. In her interchange with Jesus, she certainly was not afraid to ask penetrating questions. In fact she even pressed with some persistence to get the answers she needed. She ventured into waters she knew nothing about. It just shows that our persistence will be rewarded.

We might as well face up to the truth because Jesus Christ knows all about us. Nothing can really be hidden from him. It's beyond the time for playing games. There's no sense in putting up smoke screens. It's time to be honest with the Lord and with people in our lives. It's wisdom to confess our sins, repent of them, and rejoice in the knowledge that they are forgiven. Sins not confessed are sins that are not forgiven.

It's all right to be hungry and thirsty for spiritual truth and understanding and eternal forgiveness. It was this woman's thirst for living water that allowed her to experience a spiritual quenching of her needs by an encounter with the Messiah. In the natural, thirst is a God-given safety measure that can keep you alive and healthy. The same holds true in the spiritual.

Finally, through this woman we are taught that living water is meant to be shared and not hoarded! She couldn't keep the good news to herself. It had to be shared! It became the cup that overflowed and blessed others.

Chapter Seven

RHODA

Desperate to be believed

Rhoda was a servant, a maid, a slave girl with a Greek name meaning "a rose." She was a domestic servant to Mary, the mother of Mark the evangelist who apparently was a wealthy widow living in Jerusalem.

Mary's brother Barnabas was from Cyprus, and it's quite reasonable to believe his family had resided there for some time. It's also quite possible Barnabas brought Rhoda, who had been given a Greek name, back to Jerusalem and gave her to his sister to be a domestic in her home. Being a slave, she is not given a genealogy. And as a servant, she kept no 40-hour work week because the events that unfolded were well past midnight. There was no union time schedule for her.

Scripture: *Acts 12:1-19*

HER SIDE OF THE STORY...

I am a domestic which, in my day, really is a nice way of saying that I am a slave girl. Now don't feel sorry for me, I was one of the fortunate ones in my class. There were lots of slaves in my day; in fact, almost every wealthy household had at least one domestic. I loved my mistress, Mary. Our household was an exciting place in which to be because she was one of the wealthiest members of our new church and provided hospitality and a home to all in need. It was a wonderful time to be a small part of this growing new church entity. I was included in all the activities and our house was always full of happy guests. Our home became a beehive of activity because of the church and the ministry Mary had.

One of my most favorite guests was our pastor, Peter. He was bold and brash, fun loving and serious, loud and loving all at the same time. I just loved it when he stopped by for a meal or just to chat or to conduct a Bible study or prayer meeting. I loved him, and he always had a good word for me whenever I served him.

The news that day was not good. King Herod had captured James and had him beheaded because this pleased the unbelieving Jews. So Herod thought to take this ploy one step further by apprehending Peter and throwing him into prison. He planned to really make a spectacle having his trial right at the time of one of our celebrations—the Feast of Unleavened Bread. When Peter was in prison, what did our church do? We all went to prayer—we had numerous prayer meetings and vigils to pray for Peter's safety.

On this particular night, the prayer meeting was held in our home. It was packed with people praying. I was in my little corner and praying with all the rest. Then it seemed that it was only me who heard the knock at the outer door, probably because it was my job to keep an eye on the gate and let in guests.

I quickly ran to the outer door. Of course, in our day we never opened the door in the dark before knowing who it was that was knocking. "Who's there?" I asked.

"It's me, Peter!"

It was awesome! I knew Peter was in prison, but I recognized his voice! I was so happy that I ran back into the prayer meeting! I was so excited that I forgot to open the door for him. I ran into the middle of the main room, stumbling over people who were praying, and shouted as loud as I could, "Peter is outside!"

Were they happy to get this news? No, because they didn't believe me! They were praying for him and his release, but when it happened, they didn't believe it!

They said, "Rhoda, you're out of your mind! This is impossible! It can't be!" They really insulted me. I think you lose something in the translation of the story by Luke. They really said, "You are a raving maniac! You are a mad woman!"

But I kept on shouting, "It's him! It's Peter! I heard him talking to me!" I was really becoming emotional, but not getting through to these wonderful faith-filled believers who were praying for deliverance.

They said, "Rhoda, it must be his ghost! Maybe even his angel! It still can't be Peter! Girl, you're losing it!"

Good old Peter, he didn't give up. You should have heard the knocking. He was beating on the door until everybody heard. You probably already know this, but Peter was not a very patient guy. He was pounding on the door, shaking the house, and shouting, "Let me in!"

They went to the door this time. When they opened it and saw him they were blown away! There Peter stood in the flesh. They were speechless. They were praying for his release and when their prayers were answered, they were dumfounded. I started to laugh at the expression on their faces.

Peter waved his hand for silence, looked at me with his broad smile of approval, and shared the most exciting story I had ever heard.

"I was sleeping between two soldiers, bound to them with chains. In the night, the cell lit up, and I was punched in the side by this creature who said 'get dressed and let's go.' The cell door popped open, and the gates opened before us. This guy and I walked down the street and suddenly he just disappeared. At first I thought I was sleep walking or something. Finally it dawned on me that God had sent one of his angels to set me free, and here I am!"

I fed him a kosher corned beef on rye sandwich with pickles because he was always hungry. After wolfing it down, he said, "I've got to get out of here before they come looking for me." And with another wave of his hand, he disappeared into the night.

Then did we ever have a praise service! We gave God the glory and thanked him for answered prayer.

The next morning, the soldiers at the prison were severely interrogated. No one had ever made a successful prison break in its history. They searched every part of the town and all our houses for Peter, but he was not to be found. He was gone! King Herod was about to have a heart attack. Never had our city seen him so mad. This whole thing made him look like a fool because the word had spread everywhere as to what had happened.

Finally, King Herod, in all his pomposity, personally cross-examined the guards who didn't have an explanation as to how Peter managed his escape. So he took his wrath out on that guard unit, all 16 of them, and beheaded them in a public execution. That was sad.

But I knew what had happened, and all the church folk knew what had happened. We spread the word through the town about the powerful God we served.

I shall never in all my life forget that night even if I become an aged, old wrinkled crone. This night changed my life forever and really made me a believer in the power of prayer!

WISDOM FOR 21ST CENTURY LIVING
FROM THE LIFE OF A SERVANT WHO WAS CALLED
MAD...

There are many principles we can glean from this story, but one that stands out above the others could be called "doubt." Have you ever had to deal with your doubt when it comes to spiritual things? When you doubt, you are being uncertain about something or even believing it will not happen.

Peter had been imprisoned and the church had gone to prayer on his behalf. However, as the story unfolds, apparently while they were praying, they were doubting they would receive an answer. We can assume this because of their reactions to the news that Peter was at the front door. They accused Rhoda of being mad, but this didn't shut her up so they took another tack and said it was the ghost or angel of Peter, not Peter.

Because they prayed in spite of their doubt, they received an answer. The problem would have been if their doubt had stopped them from praying in the first place. They prayed with doubt and still received an answer. Doubt is a much bigger problem when it keeps us from prayer.

Chapter Eight

HERODIAS

Desperate for revenge

 Let's face it...this was a very bad gal! She was a bonafide, card-carrying, certified member of the Herodian dynasty, considered by some to have been the most despicable royal dynasty in all of human history! Herodias is the female form of Herod, which was the royal name for these political rulers in Christ's time.

Herodias was the daughter of Aristobulus, the son of Herod the Great and the fetching Mariamne, who was daughter of Hyrcanus. Her first marriage was to Philip I, son of Herod the Great. Yes, she married her own uncle. These two had a daughter, Salome, whom we have already discussed. When Herod Antipas made a visit to Rome, he happened to be entertained by Philip and his lovely Herodias. One thing led to another, and she divorced Philip and married Herod, his brother, and her other uncle. She managed to commit adultery and incest at the same time. She had Mariamne beheaded, as well as two of Herod's brothers.

Scripture: *Matthew 14:3-12; Mark 6:14-29; Luke 3:19-20*

HER SIDE OF THE STORY...

I was really bad and proud of it! I was a part of the Herod

dynasty, and I didn't care one bit what others might think of me. I was vile and vicious, one of the most infamous women in history. Fortunately, I was also beautiful, which certainly helped. There is only one other woman in the whole world to rival my beauty, and her I desperately hate and would kill if I had a chance—Cleopatra.

I was young when I married old Uncle Philip. I thought he was quite a catch. You need to understand that our entire family was so enamored with who we were that no one else outside of the family was good enough for any of us to marry. Naturally, then, we married each other. "Keep the goods in the family," we always said. Soon, to my great disappointment, I discovered old Uncle Phil was not much of a lover. There was not much life left in him, but the perks of living with a king were something else, however. So I put up with the old guy as long as I could stand him.

Then we got word that Phil's younger brother and his lovely wife were coming to Rome, and it would be our privilege to host their visit. I didn't think too much about this until they arrived. Wow! I did a double take. Herod was some kind of a hunk—younger, better looking, and most importantly, more powerful than dear old Phil. He laid those dark browns on me for the first time and raised his eyebrows in surprise—his little niece had grown up and was a knock-out! I immediately saw that he took notice of me.

"Let the games begin!" was my battle cry. It was every woman for herself. I knew exactly how to play the game. There was one little detail—the beautiful Arabian princess who happened to be the current queen. No problem, Herod saw the light and divorced her, and with my insistence, later had her beheaded. Too bad...so sad. And Herod took me as his queen, stolen right away from his brother Phil. That was nasty, but somehow Herod made a kind of an out-of-court settlement and off we went—the king and queen in Jerusalem! I was quite proud of my coup: incest and adultery at the same time. It's more sordid than any of your current movie plots.

You'll also enjoy this tidbit: the name "Herod" and my female version "Herodias" meant "heroic." That was a family joke—we weren't heroic, we were hellish! It was always good for laughs at any kind of family get-together.

Life for me and my striking daughter and new husband, went along nicely until this weird guy named John started making noises. Would you believe he lived on bugs, grasshoppers, and honey and dressed in wild animal skins? He never shaved and had the biggest mop of wild hair you've ever seen—but there was something about his eyes! He was the latest evangelist to come on the scene. Everywhere he went, he gathered a huge crowd. The people loved him, but I couldn't figure out why.

He baptized people in the muddy river and preached about sin and repentance. You could hear him preaching a mile away; he had a fog horn for a voice. He was a phenomenon to be reckoned with because the people flocked to hear him and followed him.

But worse than that, my lovely husband began to be taken with this guy. He didn't always understand his message, but he liked to listen to him preach. And preach he did—always about sin and repentance and baptism. A simple, but effective message. In fact, we royalty began to be fearful of what this guy could do in leading the hungry masses against us.

Then what I heard from his mouth next made me really mad! "Herod, you are a guilty sinner! You are living with your brother's wife and that is against the law of God and the laws of man! You and your wife are on the way to hell!" This could cause me to lose my lovely palace and powerful husband.

John's rantings went on for day after day, but Herod continued to be fascinated by the man. I had to stop this nonsense and quickly! I attempted to have this man killed but somehow couldn't get it done. In fact, Herod arrested John and put him into prison so I couldn't get at him. Often, my lovely, naïve Herod would visit John in his prison. He was puzzled by a whole lot of what John said, but John always zeroed in on me and our relationship. It drove me nuts! Soon it came down to Herod choosing either him or me. I hated John, so I plotted, planned, and schemed for his demise. I wanted air between his head and shoulders one way or another.

Unfortunately Herod was deathly afraid of this man and his power. Herod argued with me and called him a "just man" and said, "I'd gladly listen to him rather than to you any day." That just added fuel to the fire as far as I was concerned. We fought bitterly over John, with Herod defending him, and I attacking him.

I shouted at my man, "If it's the last thing I do in this life, I will kill John the Baptist!"

But how was I to do this? Talk about something being the perfect set up! Birthdays are always celebrated riotously in our family. Herod's was coming up soon, and already preparations were being made for the biggest bash of the year. It was to be a huge stag party with free drinks for everybody. Here was my opportunity. John was as good as dead—let the good times roll!

I could almost taste the sweet joy of revenge! I knew my plan would work because I knew my lusty husband. I have a daughter, Salome, and she is hot. I knew the combination would work to perfection.

Today's courts would call it pre-meditated murder, but, re-member, we Herods were above the law. No one could touch us. And it all came together on his birthday!

The day arrived, and I could hardly keep that happy smirk

off my face, but I didn't dare tip my hand ahead of time. Salome had been clued in to my plan and dressed in a gauzy outfit that showed off all her fine points, if you know what I mean. I had her practice her erotic and sensual dance several times that day. Remember, it was a stag party with no women allowed. The drinks were flowing freely, and the blue-bloods were having a great time. In case you're thinking this was no place for a young princess, you're right. But I didn't care. I'd use anybody and any tactic to get the man John—even my innocent daughter. So give me a minus ten on motherhood.

Just when this party was really moving, I sent in my little Salome. She slunk to center stage, right in front of her stepdad, with hips swinging and gyrating, and danced her little heart out. (You should also know that good girls in my day never danced in public. Period. But this was a special occasion.) The place just about came apart—you should have heard the hoots and whistles and catcalls!

I watched Herod, who happened to be the most intent. He was flushed in the face and well on his way to being roaring drunk. She had created the right effect!

She "pleased" her stepdad...did he ever approve. She made her step-daddy so happy he wanted to reward her.

"Honey," he said with a slur, "ask me for anything...anything! I mean it. I really mean it...you can have anything up to half my kingdom!" Yeah, girl, go for it! Exactly!

She turned to look for me and came running, "Mom, what should I ask for?" This lusty crowd was shouting for an encore and when she returned to the front after getting my directions, they thought that was what was coming. The place became dead silent. The effect was just right...Salome had learned well, and her timing was exquisite.

"Well, honey, what will it be?"

"The head of John the Baptist on a platter!"

Not only did I want him dead, I wanted him disgraced so that word would spread, "Do not mess with Herodias!"

You could hear the gasps of surprise from the now too quiet stag party. Herod was stunned! He blanched white with fear!

Before he could recover, Salome told him firmly, "I want his head right now!" I thought it was a very nice touch. I would have been content with a public execution the next day, but she really came through. A daughter just like her mother. What a team we made!

Herod was up to his ears in a very big problem with all the bigshots of the realm looking at him. I knew his pride and his need for public approval would win out over what was the right thing to do. I could read the pain in his face—he'd been caught like a rat in a trap with no way out. He was forced to save face, somehow, and carry out his promise.

Of course this was in defiance of Jewish law, which prohibited execution without a trial. Did I care? Did Herod care about the law? Hardly! We are Herods and always above the law.

Herod sent for the number one head chopper in his kingdom—the one with a large scimitar—and dispatched him to bring back John's head. It didn't take long. Every eye was focused on the door.

With a flourish and a bow, the executioner presented the platter with John's head to Salome. Did she really want to take a look? The stare of death was in his wide open eyes, his hair and beard was splashed in gore and blood. Many of the partygoers fainted dead away when the blood began dripping off the platter.

Salome gingerly took the platter with a look of disgust and quickly brought it to me as if she were holding a hot pan.

I placed the platter on my lap and reached up for a hair pin, about six inches long. I pulled his tongue out and plunged the pin through the tongue that had challenged my lifestyle. What satisfaction! How sweet is revenge! Needless to say, the party was over. The fat lady didn't sing, but the vile one—that's me—did a victory dance!

I kept the head for a trophy and mounted it where I could see it often. The disciples of John came and buried his body, without the head.

Did this affect me? Not really, at the time. But I have to admit that I was subjected to nightmares the rest of my life. Salome never did really come out of it. She went into a deep depression and became suicidal, poor baby. Finally she went stark, raving mad, and we had to have her put away.

As for Herod, his guilt was overwhelming. He never recovered nor did he ever forgive me for my subterfuge. He had trouble sleeping. He was almost like a man who was driven with fear. He was impossible to live with. But I must tell you that when Jesus began his ministry, Herod was positive John had been raised from the dead and came back to haunt him.

As for me I was still ambitious and kept pushing my husband. We became so obnoxious that eventually we were banished from the land of Israel and sent to Gaul! This was like being sent to Siberia, the absolute armpit of the empire.

I think I know what you are thinking, "She needed to pay for this!" But my head stayed on my shoulders, and I died a natural death. And I never did repent, I never did relent, and to my dying day, I was proud to have put an end to this John!

I hope you remember me in your 21st century culture as the meanest, most vicious woman in all of the Bible! If there is a nastier woman than me, I'd like to meet her. I'm proud of my life and history.

Hell gladly welcomed me with open arms. My life was eaten up with anger, hatred, bitterness, cruelty, vileness, evil, and vengeance right to the end. You see, I created my own kind of hell right here on earth.

WISDOM FOR 21ST CENTURY LIVING
FROM THE LIFE OF THE BIBLE'S WORST EXAMPLE...

Let's begin with the obvious...if someone (including your pastor or best friend) points out your sin, please don't chop their head off! Most of us do not take kindly to correction, but if we are wrong, we need to admit it and begin doing the right thing.

Too much people-pleasing can get you in deep trouble. Herod made a promise because he was pleased with his step-daughter. He paid dearly for being so rash and caused an innocent man to die.

Deal with your anger before it turns into a plan of revenge. Revenge belongs to the Lord.

Chapter Nine

MARY, THE MOTHER OF JESUS

No desperation in her life!

 To write about this lady presents the most difficult assignment for an author. No other female in human history is as well known as she. More has been written about her than any other woman by well-known theologians, songwriters, poets, preachers, prophets—and just common writers like me. There is nothing I can add that will enhance or reduce her as she is known world-wide. So, I humbly present my input.

The name "Mary" in its Hebrew form means "bitterness" or even "trouble and sorrow." Mary is the name of more women in America than any other as well as being the number one name for girls in other Christian nations. There are at least 70 different interpretations such as, Maria, Marie, Miriam, and more. Mary is one of the very few female names that also have masculine forms like Mario, Marion, and so on. Mary the Virgin, whom we will be taking another look at, truly had a number of "bitter" experiences.

Scripture: *Matthew 1; 2; 12:46; Luke 1; 2; John 2:1-11; 19:25; Acts 1:14*

HER SIDE OF THE STORY...

My life was suddenly and completely changed when the

angel Gabriel made a visit to me, a humble peasant Jewish girl. There were lots of other wonderful Jewish girls. Why me?

Gabriel told me, "You are highly favored! The Lord is with you!"

Wouldn't you be surprised and a bit upset with such an announcement? What kind of a greeting was this; what did it mean? Before I could think of a reply, the angel went on, "You have found favor with the Lord, and you will give birth to his one and only Son! He will be the greatest person to ever live on this earth! And his kingdom will never end!" How can I describe my overwhelming sense of awe?

Finally I found my tongue, "How can this be since I am a virgin?"

Gabriel replied, "This is the work of the Holy Spirit in you!"

He had more to say. "Your cousin, Elizabeth, will also have a miracle child; she's in her sixth month even though she's beyond child-bearing age." What incredible news—our entire family knew how much she had wanted to give birth. But the angel wasn't through, he continued, "Nothing is impossible with God!" I knew that, in theory, but these two announcements brought this truth to reality!

You know my story, so I'll not go into every detail but only select a few highlights. My engaged spouse, Joseph, had to be convinced, so when the angel also appeared to him, he too became a believer! What a man my Joseph was! He was the perfect male model for my Jesus. You know it's too bad that more wasn't written about him. By the time the writers of the New Testament were recording the works of Jesus, he had already died. None of them knew him, which was too bad. Take it from me, Joseph was God's special choice for the task of being the male image in the life of my sons and daughters. I sure missed him. He would have been so proud of Jesus, but by the time Jesus began his ministry, he was gone.

So how do you raise the Son of God? We decided to treat him like the rest of our kids—he had four brothers, James, Joses, Judas, and Simon, and sisters, who did not get named in the New Testament record. Since Jesus was the first born, he had the unique responsibilities of the oldest son in a typical Jewish home. He learned the family trade—carpentry. He became the best in our village, most said.

Jesus was a quick learner and a model, obedient child in every way, except for one time! He was supposed to have been travelling back with us from Jerusalem, but instead he stayed behind and we later found him preaching in the Temple to men who were three times his age! If that didn't show our family that he was different, I don't know what would.

I eagerly watched him mature into a responsible adult. Life wasn't always easy for him. He was a studious son—he devoured the writings of the Fathers from scroll to scroll. Like most Jewish young men, he memorized the first five books of the Bible. There was something special about the way he prayed and communed with our heavenly Father.

I kept these things in my heart and pondered on them. What did they mean? How and when would he begin his life's work? We had many long chats, just the two of us, often in the shade of a tree at the mid-day break or in a long walk in the cool of the evening. He bounced all kinds of things off me—things he didn't understand and was working out.

After he changed the water into wine at the wedding feast at my request, he gently hugged me and whispered, "Mother, it's time for me to begin my ministry. My brothers will have to take care of you. It's time for me to go public and present our heavenly Father to this world. I must be about his business. I love you. I thank you. Blessings…" And he was gone from my home, forever.

News filtered back as to the miraculous things that happened when he taught and preached and prayed for people. Healings, deliverances, and provisions happened quite regularly. Soon, I decided it was time for me to join his followers and become a strong encourager and help with the ministry. There was so much to do to feed him and his twelve. What a bunch they were—imagine 13 hungry guys traipsing around the countryside. They had all bought into his mission and ministry—what a wonderful time those three short years were!

One of the hurts of being his mother was the way in which his brothers and sisters refused to follow and believe in him. They didn't believe in him nor his mission until after his death and resurrection. So there was ridicule from his own siblings, and that's never easy to take. Then there were the neighbors and townspeople. My heart broke for him many times, the mocking could be so brutal. But I had been convinced by the angel Gabriel of who he was before he was born. Oh, there were times when I had my doubts, but seeing him in action convinced me that he truly was the Son of God! He would be the one to change this world. He was the promised Messiah.

Like many of his followers, I believed he would set up his kingdom and overthrow the bondages of the Roman Empire! It wasn't to be. The disappointment was palpable. Why didn't he set his kingdom up on this earth during our time? Later I finally realized that the kingdom of God was to be born in human hearts. He came to set the captives—those who were bound in unbelief, fear, and sin—free! He came to bring liberty to all mankind.

The angel had promised that my heart would be pierced through with a sword of sorrow. I had many disappointments and bitter happenings along the way, but nothing compared to watching his last week of life. When he came riding into Jerusalem in a triumphal entry, I was sure this would be the time he would be crowned king, but it didn't happen.

The agony of watching his beatings and humiliation was more than I could bear—I had to look away. Imagine watching your first-born subjected to this kind of pain. The climb to the top of the Golgatha hill was beyond heart-breaking. He had become weakened by the beatings until he couldn't carry his cross. I would have gladly carried it and would have even taken his place, but it was not to be.

Those six hours of the crucifixion were agonizing. Yet, even when facing a certain death, he thought about me and told John to take care of me. Not my other sons, but John, his closest associate.

Then it was all over! He was dead! I had no way to take care of his body. Thank God, Joseph of Arimathea stepped forward and helped Nicodemus wrap my son's body in linen and lay him in a nearby new tomb which had never been used. We women watched from a distance as he was laid inside; there was a finality when the stone was rolled over the opening. Sadly we all turned away; we had the Sabbath to observe. It was over! All our hopes and dreams were seemingly dashed. Now what? The least we could do was to prepare spices and perfumes for a proper burial.

Early in the morning of the first day of the week, while it was still dark, we women made our way to the tomb. One question bothered all of us: Who was strong enough to roll away the stone which had been set to seal the tomb by the Roman guards? Surprise of all surprises! When we arrived, the stone was already rolled away, and the tomb was empty! Angels were sitting on the stone! Angels in white! (Remember, I know an angel when I see one.)

It had all happened so suddenly that we hardly had time to process the events. We went from the depths of despair to the heights of joy on a roller coaster ride such as nobody has ever experienced.

We all ran back to tell the eleven disciples, who had gone into hiding because they were afraid they would be crucified next. They didn't believe us! They accused us of being out of our minds and speaking nonsense.

Finally, Peter and John were prodded into action. John was faster and beat Peter to the tomb, but he wasn't bold enough to go in by himself. When they both went in and saw the empty tomb, at first they didn't know what had happened! They still didn't believe the words of Jesus when he had promised that he would die and rise again!

They ran back and while they were expounding on all that had happened, Jesus himself appeared in the room where they were hiding!

"Peace!" he said.

They were startled and thought he was a ghost!

Then he said, "Touch me." Which they did, but still didn't believe.

He said, "Give me some fish to eat." They were dumfounded and amazed, and still didn't believe.

Finally, he opened their minds and got through to them. "This is exactly what I told you. I would be killed and after three days come back from the dead." Finally, it dawned on them that he was alive, and they would be his witnesses in all the world to the most fantastic event in all of human history!

Well, finally my other children believed. James became one of the first to pastor our church and also one of the first martyrs. Need I tell you that the day of Pentecost was the next most wonderful day in my entire life? The church was born in a day!

My life was spent witnessing to my son's powerful, life-giving life. I lived to a ripe old age, serving others and enjoying the fruits of his labor—a life that changed the world. It's amazing to think that it all began with me, a peasant girl, who was favored of the Lord.

There's not much more to say…my life was all about Jesus. And you well know the rest of my story as well as the rest of his story.

WISDOM FOR 21ST CENTURY LIVING
FROM THE MOTHER OF OUR LORD…

When Mary went to spend time with her cousin Elizabeth, she sang a song which is called the "Magnificat." This was followed by the song of Zacharias named the "Benedictus." At the temple ceremony, Simeon sang what is known as the "Nunc Dimittis." The angels had shouted "Glory to God in the Highest." But the most remarkable of these is Mary's "Magnificat." This has been called "the most inspiring song from the heart of a woman that has ever been written" (Edith Deen).

Let's read it from the very words of Mary…a teen when these were spoken:

My soul glorifies the Lord,
And my spirit rejoices in God my Savior,
For He has been mindful of the humble state of his servant.
From now on all generations will call me blessed,
For the Mighty One has done great things for me.
Holy is His name.
His mercy extends to those who fear him,
    from generation to generation.
He has performed mighty deeds with his arm;
He has scattered those who are proud
    in their inmost thoughts.
He has brought down rulers from their thrones
But has lifted up the humble.
He has filled the hungry with good things
But has sent the rich away empty.

He has helped his servant Israel,
Remembering to be merciful to Abraham
  and his descendants forever,
Even as He said to our fathers!
(Luke 1:46-55)

Chapter Ten

MARY MAGDALENE

Desperate for deliverance

 Next to the mother of Jesus, Mary Magdalene is likely the second most recognized Mary in the world. But let's set the record straight right up front. She has mistakenly been pictured as a prostitute and profligate type of woman by many writers and even by the Church many times. The Bible doesn't say anything about this, it only mentions that she had been possessed by seven demons but nothing of her supposed sordid lifestyle is given.

Yes, the record does state that she was possessed by seven demons, and this may have manifested itself as a serious mental or even a physical illness from which Jesus delivered her. Nothing is given us about her lineage or marital status or family status. It states simply that she was a resident of Magdala, a prosperous Galilean coastal city. Likely she had some wealth or at least had no attachments that prevented her from being part of Jesus' entourage for about three years.

Scripture: *Matthew 27:56, 61; 28:1; Mark 15:40-47; 16:1-19; Luke 8:2; 24:10; John 19:25; 20:1-18*

HER SIDE OF THE STORY...

I awoke long before dawn and lay in bed with my tortured

mind and body, preparing for another dreadful day. My life to this point had been a nightmare. I was tormented day and night, and nothing I did ever relieved the pressures for long. Because of my condition I was never able to be loved or wanted by a man. Who wanted to live with a tormented woman? I was given to seizures—uncontrollable things that sometimes threw me to the ground in writhing agony. My family had taken me to doctors, but no one could help me.

There were times when I didn't seem to be in my right mind, and this could strike me at the most embarrassing times. It was impossible for me to be in public. The whole community knew about me: Mary the Possessed One. Even attending any temple ceremonies could be a problem. Fortunately my family had the means to provide the best care available in our area, but nothing that was done for me helped for any length of time. I was deeply depressed. Physically, I looked a wreck—even my hair was sickly looking. My eyes were deeply set and my cheeks sunken. I was undernourished and a walking skeleton. It was awful. I couldn't bear to look at myself in the mirror. Why was I like this? Did I inherit something bad? Nobody else in my family was plagued as I was.

But today was the day I would be changed forever! We had been hearing rumors about the wonderful rabbi who went about doing good, healing sick folk, and delivering people from all kinds of bondages. The buzz of this day was that he would make a visit to our town. My parents were planning to bring me to his meetings in hopes of getting some help for me. I was excited—for the first time in my miserable life, a faint glimmer of hope began to burn.

Some of the kids began running up and down our streets shouting, "He's here. Come and see the rabbi!"

Quickly my parents and I made our way to the edge of town with the rest of the crowd. I sensed something I had never sensed before—a moving inside, like my demons began to churn. The turmoil on my inside grew more agitated the closer we got to this rabbi. He was teaching truths we had never heard—positive, uplifting, enlightening and hopeful ones.

Jesus paused and began praying for all who were sick and afflicted. There were shouts of joy because the most incredible things were happening. Neighbors who were crippled instantly began walking normally, in fact they were running about. An elderly lady who was bent way over straightened up. A neighbor born deaf declared he could hear. A little girl who was born with crippled legs was healed and squealed in joy as she tried out her perfect, new legs. It was unbelievable!

Person after person was made complete—every one whom he prayed for was helped! Hope became alive in my spirit, and the demons became more agitated. My headache was absolutely unbearable when my parents pushed me toward Jesus. They finally carried me the last bit because my legs gave out.

And wouldn't you know it, the Master gently looked at me and the demons inside threw me to the ground and defied the rabbi. Through my lips they shouted at him, "She is ours! We possessed her!"

He commanded them to shut up and then to leave and return to the pit from where they had come! It was instantaneous! In the blink of an eye, I was set free!

There are no words I can tell you to convince you of what had happened inside. I felt clean. I felt like the heavy burden in my body had been taken away. My thoughts were no longer jumbled. I felt like something had scrubbed out my insides. I felt like I was walking on air and wanted to shout with joy! I looked at the Master and knew I would follow him all the rest of my days because he had set me free. My thoughts were finally clear, and I could reason once again. There was no more headache pain. It was unbelievably awesome!

My family grabbed me and did a Jewish dance right there—the whole town was touched by this man. Most of them decided to follow and believe in this miracle-worker sent from God.

My mother held my face in her hands and said, "Honey, I see the sparkle of happiness in your eyes. Even your cheeks are glowing with something special inside. Your body is as though it is new—you are a new creature!" She hugged me tightly and rejoiced. "I have a new daughter!" What a day!

I declared my faith in this rabbi. It was as though God in human flesh had come to bless us. I declared I would do anything out of my gratitude to help in his further ministry. I wanted the world to hear my story...me—"The Magdalene"— out of whom seven demons were cast away. That's when my life really began.

I immediately volunteered to be a part of the support group. In order for this ministry to continue, a number of us women did the cooking and the laundry, made arrangements for places to stay, and did anything else to relieve the burden of the mundane from Jesus so his ministry could be shared with our people all across Israel. What a time! Even the mother of Jesus was part of our group. I asked her all about him. I just couldn't get enough of his wisdom and teaching and seeing the miracles happen.

I left my comfortable home to travel with the happiest band of people in the entire world. We women provided from our own supply of money so Jesus and his men never asked for money. It was our happy privilege.

The stories I could tell would fill a really huge book. So much of what happened in those three short years never did get told. But it all came to a screeching halt when Jesus was arrested and put on trial—a highly illegal trial at that—and condemned to die. I watched it all from a short distance away, and with the other women I followed as he walked up the hill to be crucified. We wept at the injustice and cruelty and mocking that was heaped upon this man. He was the most gentle, loving, caring, compassionate man who ever walked this earth. Yet when it was required, he could be masculine in the best sense of the word. He was the most complete human being I had ever met—perfectly balanced, the human and the divine. They wanted to kill him and silence his teachings because they feared him and his followers.

We watched through those most agonizing six hours as he hung on the cross. Crucifixion was a Roman specialty, a cruelty of the highest order. Everything about being crucified was humiliating, degrading, painful, and intended to be a warning for any other law breaker. Jesus, who had never broken any laws, was killed like any other common criminal. He who had done nothing but good was silenced forever, or so they thought.

After he died, I made my way to the foot of the cross and knelt in a final farewell. My heart was breaking. I watched as Joseph and Nicodemus took his body away and followed behind as they put him in a tomb. It was a hurry-up thing because the Sabbath had to be observed. He was wrapped in linen and the stone was rolled across the tomb. The soldiers were stationed to guard the tomb and his dead body. Then we all left.

We women got our heads together and planned to buy spices and perfumes and return after the Sabbath was over and finish the preparation of his body for the final resting. This particular Sabbath was the saddest day of my life—how was life to go on now that he was dead? His life that had brought so much hope and love and healing to the hurting was silenced. What next? The future was bleak to say the least.

None of us could sleep that night, and so, very early, before light, we gathered our spices and perfumes and made our way to the tomb. It was to be our last labor of love for this man whom we had followed and believed.

When we got there, the stone was rolled away and we could see inside in the early dawn. I looked in, and it was empty! There was no body—no Jesus! There were just his body wraps lying empty inside. What did it mean? My first thought was that this was the work of a body-snatcher. Who would do such a thing? Was this another insult from Herod?

Immediately I ran back into town. Being younger than the other women, I found Peter first and told him, "He's gone! They've taken him away!"

Peter and I ran back...Peter took a look, shook his head, and went back into Jerusalem. I stayed. I don't know why. I just wanted to be there where he had last been. Maybe it was a final act of devotion to simply sit and wait. Wait for what? I didn't know.

I was weeping like a silly woman. Then, I bent down and looked inside once more. To my surprise, two creatures (later I realized they were angels) in shiny white sat, one at either end of the stony platform on which he had been lying.

They spoke, "Woman, why are you crying?"

My incredulous answer was, "They have taken my Lord away, and I don't know where they are hiding him!"

A slight movement caught my eye and I turned. There was another man that I decided was the gardener. I figured that he'd know what had happened.

"Sir, if you have carried Jesus' body away, tell me where you are hiding him and I will get him!" I figured that I would finish his embalming—it would be my last act of love. As I waited for his answer, I looked a bit closer into his eyes.

"Mary!" he gently spoke my name!

"Rabboni!" I shouted. It was him—the Teacher, the Master, the Healer, the Son of God! It was him—somehow, he was alive!

I fell to my knees in an act of worship! I reached for his feet to simply touch him. Imagine...he could have appeared first to King Herod or Pontius Pilate or the High Priest or in the Temple or to his male disciples. But he appeared to me, a woman whose testimony in court would have meant nothing in my day. He appeared to me—a woman whose love propelled me to the cross and then to the grave; a woman out of whom he banished seven demons; a woman who was now in her right mind and would love and serve him forever! It was one of the highest privileges in all of human history to be the first one he appeared to after his resurrection! Isn't it amazing, at his birth he appeared to humble shepherds and was born into a peasant family, and at his resurrection he revealed himself to a lowly woman!

I was thrilled and excited beyond words. Then he said, "Mary, you can't touch me because I must go to my heavenly Father and I'll be back."

Naturally, with my heart pounding nearly out of my chest, I tracked down the disciples and told them, "He's alive! I saw him! I talked to him! He talked to me!" Did they believe? Hardly. Oh well, I knew that Jesus lived again! This man was alive! I lived long enough to tell and retell my story in our new church to any and all who would listen to me. If he could use me like this, surely he can use you, too.

WISDOM FOR 21ST CENTURY LIVING
FROM THE LIFE OF MARY MAGDALENE...

Jesus knew all about this woman—everything about her past, her present and her wonderful potential after she had been set free. She became a follower and suffered with him through the agony of his last days.

In the same way He knows the same about each of us. When life is empty and hope is gone, he cares. Maybe others have let you down, but Jesus calls you and me by name. The ultimate outcome of an encounter with him is much like Mary's—she was filled with joy and so can we be.

Another lesson from the life of Mary is that all the world can see what Christ is able to do for a woman or anybody else. She was cleansed and set free! She had been afflicted and tormented and when set free was a loving follower. She was changed from a sinner into a saint! She was set free from bondage into freedom! He can do the same for you!

And look what she was able to do for Jesus and the Kingdom of God. Her life became one of giving, sacrifice, and care. The gratitude Mary had for her Lord manifested itself in practical ways as she appreciated all he had done for her.

Chapter Eleven

MARY OF BETHANY

Desperate to learn

 There are six different women named Mary in the New Testament: Mary the mother of Jesus, Mary Magdalene, Mary of Bethany, Mary the mother of James and Joses, Mary the mother of John Mark, and Mary of Rome. Sometimes their stories and lives are mingled together. And this is the last Mary we will read about.

Little is known about her background other than she was the sister of Martha and Lazarus in the town of Bethany. Their home was known for hospitality, and they must have had a bit of wealth because of this home and the huge gift she was eventurally going to bestow on Jesus.

Scripture: *Matthew 26:6-13; Mark 14:3-9; Luke 10:38-42; John 11:1-12:1-3*

HER SIDE OF THE STORY...

It was unusual for three siblings to live together. Our parents had died before we were of marrying age, and we were raised by an aunt who took us in. Fortunately, all the land, house, and holdings were passed on to Lazarus our brother because he was the only son. But Lazarus never married, and instead, chose to make a home for Martha and I. Ours was a happy lifestyle. We had a large, wonderful home. We loved to entertain all kinds of people—travelers, friends, family, whoever.

Everybody had heard of Jesus' reputation. We made friends with him and his followers, and offered our home to them any time they came our way. Our house was like a retreat for him, a place to get away from the crowds that thronged him. We learned to love him and his twelve disciples. And could they ever put the food away! It seemed these guys were always hungry, what with living outdoors and their strenuous schedule. We made our house a special place of hiding and relaxation for them, especially for the Master. In fact, we had prepared a special room for him. We loved it every time they stopped, and they stopped frequently. I think it was because of our hospitality and the great cooking that my sister, Martha, did. There's nothing like good home cooking.

I'm sort of famous for three events that centered about the Master.

I loved to learn! I had attended all the schooling that was possible for a girl in my day. Boys went to school much longer than we girls did. It wasn't fair, but I made the best of it. After my meager schooling, I devoured every bit of reading material I could get my hands on. I would sneak in the back of the temple or synagogue where the boys were being taught, and listened to the rabbi teach them. Learning was my passion.

Jesus was my favorite visitor. I loved to be with him, and I loved to hear him teach. He shared concepts never before heard in our nation. I was like a sponge. And as often as I could get away, I was part of the crowd who gathered to hear him preach and watch him heal.

On one particular visit, my sister Martha was scurrying around getting dinner ready for Jesus and his twelve and some friends who had also dropped in on us. You couldn't just send them all away without feeding them. It was a load for Martha, I could tell. Finally, she stopped in front of Jesus, with hands on her hips and said, "I need her help!"

He gently looked at Martha and replied, "Martha, Martha, don't be so bothered about cooking and cleaning. You worry too much. I know what you do is important, but Mary has made the best choice." Somehow the dinner got cooked and served that night. Jesus got me off the hook, but I'll have you know, I always pitched in to help.

The next event was so tragic. One day our brother Lazarus became ill and suddenly died. Where was Jesus when we needed him? We sent word for him to come; if he had been there we were sure he could have healed him and prevented his death. We buried Lazarus in the family tomb and rolled a stone over the entrance. It was a typical gravesite in our day for well-to-do families.

Jesus had gotten word about Lazarus' illness, but delayed his coming. Four long agonizing days later, after Lazarus had already been buried, Jesus came to our home. We were all crying and mourning, along with family and friends.

When Martha ran to meet Jesus, I stayed behind in the house, deep in my sorrow and grief. Martha said to Jesus, "Where have you been? If you'd been here, he wouldn't be dead."

Jesus gently replied, "Lazarus will live again!"

She answered, "We know that he'll rise in the last day in the resurrection."

Again, Jesus said, "You don't get it—I am the resurrection and the life!" Now that was astounding! He continued, "Everyone who believes in me will never die! Martha, do you believe this?"

"Yes, Lord," she told him, "I believe you are the Christ, the Son of God come in human flesh."

Then Martha came to get me, "Mary, the Teacher is here—he's asking for you."

I quickly dried my tears and ran out the door. I knelt at his feet and started crying all over again, "Lord, if you had been here, Lazarus would not have died." I couldn't help accusing him; I was so devastated by my brother's death.

"Where is he?"

"Come over here and see the tomb," I replied.

And then Jesus wept! Why? Because he loved Lazarus too? Or because of the difficulty of getting through to two thick-headed, opinionated sisters? Or because nobody in this crowd believed Lazarus could be raised from the dead?

"Take away the stone," Jesus commanded.

"But, Lord, after four days, he stinks because he is dead!" said Martha.

Patiently, Jesus went on, "Didn't I just tell you that if you believed, you would see the glory of God?"

Finally they took away the stone.

Jesus prayed a 30-second prayer for our benefit, "That they may believe you sent me!"

You should have been there with us; it was astounding. Jesus shouted into the tomb, "Lazarus, come out!" I had this strange feeling that if he hadn't specified Lazarus only, all of the dead in our cemetery would have risen.

Out came Lazarus, all wrapped up like a mummy! We were ecstatic! We could hardly believe our eyes—it really was Lazarus.

"Take off the grave wrappings; get him loose and let him go!" Our hands were shaking with joy so much we barely got them off. The first thing our brother did was to give me and Martha a great big hug and then said, "I'm hungry, got something to eat?"

The celebration which followed was one huge, happy

party! Jesus and Lazarus were the center attraction. People kept asking Lazarus, "Are you really real? Can I touch you? Can you feel? Are you a real human or are you a spirit? What was it like to be dead four days?" The questions went on and on. In fact, everywhere we went, we were questioned about Lazarus. Whenever he went out in public, people flocked around him.

There is one more event...a very special, meaningful one for me. Jesus was again visiting our home, in fact just six days before the huge upcoming Passover Feast. There would soon be at least 100,000 visitors or more in Jerusalem. It was the biggest event of the year, and this year promised to be even larger because of Jesus.

He stopped at our home for another of Martha's special home cooked meals and a bit of rest before the activities of the Passover. It was to be a dinner given in honor of Jesus. I must say, we outdid ourselves in preparing for this time.

I had made a secret plan—nobody knew about it, except me. I had been saving and planning. What could I do for Jesus that would be something out of the ordinary? I decided I needed to give him a gift worthy of who he was—a gift that really represented all of our love for him. It was to be an expression of how I felt about the changes in my life and especially how grateful our family was for the miracle of my brother, Lazarus. I waited for the perfect time and place to present this gift of love.

Martha had served the main courses of the meal. The guests were reclining (we had these special couches, a bit raised at one end on which you rested your upper body and extended your feet) about the table, talking, sharing, laughing. It was just a warm and friendly meal, but an Eastern affair—long and drawn out.

Carefully, I went to my room and retrieved my gift—a pint

of pure nard, the most expensive perfume of our day. It had cost me the typical working person's annual salary and was to be my love offering. The guests grew quiet when I entered the room carrying this precious perfume because the fragrance was readily evident.

In love and humility I knelt at his feet and tenderly poured it all out on the feet of Jesus. Then I let down my hair and wiped his feet with it. I was weeping in joy at being able to give such a gift of love. The fragrance filled the house. It was one of the most sacred and precious moments of my entire life.

Judas, pompous, greedy Judas protested, "Why didn't you sell this and give the money to the poor?" Everybody knew he was a thief, including Jesus, who tolerated him as part of the group. He controlled the money bag, and we knew he dipped into it to squander it on himself.

Jesus replied, "Leave her alone. She planned to anoint my body at burial but gave it to me now, while I'm still alive." He looked at me with approval in his compassionate eyes. Then he said the most surprising thing—the poor would always be with us, but one of these days he would be gone. And even more surprising, he said my gift of love would be shared wherever the gospel was to be preached as a memorial to him.

I was thrilled to have had the opportunity to give my gift of love before his death. But it didn't end there! We went from despair and sorrow to joy and gladness after his death and resurrection.

The three of us, Martha, Lazarus and I served the Lord the rest of our days! Christ made the difference.

WISDOM FOR 21ST CENTURY LIVING
FROM THE LIFE OF MARY OF BETHANY...

She has chosen the best things...is what Jesus said about her? Why? Her priorities were in order. She placed a high value on being in the presence of the Master of Life. She was hungry for life-giving truth and deeply devoted to Christ. What an example for all of us.

The gift of precious "pure nard" represented her well. Again, she chose wisely and prepared ahead of time. King David said it best, "I will not give a gift that has little or no cost to it."

Mary of Bethany...what a mentor for women of today!

Chapter Twelve

LUKE'S LADY

Desperate to be forgiven

 Like so many of the Bible's "nameless" women, we really know nothing of this lady's background other than she apparently was a well known sinner of the worst order. Let's face it—all women, since Eve, the world's first sinner, were born in sin and are sinners by birth. And the same holds true for all men.

You may also question my use of the term "lady" in the title. But when she met Jesus, she began a whole new life, a new start, a new day. So let's call her a lady...a forgiven lady.

Women were extremely dependent upon a husband or father for their sustenance in Jesus' time. If divorce or widowhood or other tragedy overtook them, there was no social safety net. Therefore many joined the world's "oldest profession" to sustain life. It was sad but true.

Scripture: *Luke 7:36-50*

HER SIDE OF THE STORY...

I'll admit it...I was a notorious sinner and the holier-than-thou types never let me forget it! Life for me began the same as with most good Jewish girls. But in my early teens that all changed. You see I was abused sexually by my mother's uncle and became damaged goods. He threatened me with real harm if I ever told anyone so I kept my mouth shut and crammed all those feelings deep inside.

My marriage was a full-blown disaster. I just couldn't bring myself to love my husband, even though he was a good man. He never could understand my reactions to him. I couldn't help myself. I loathed myself...I always felt dirty. I didn't blame him when I left.

I tried a second marriage, and that time I was hooked to a real loser. My attitude about myself just went further down the sewer. I tried to be a good wife, but it was no use. I patiently attempted to explain to him that the problem wasn't him but me. My self-esteem really hit bottom so I left him.

What was I to do—I hated myself and hated all men. I wanted to hurt them so I became a prostitute. At first, because of my charm and beauty, I was a highly paid night-walker. Business was good, and the pay was exceptional. Not one of the men was someone I could respect. Inwardly I laughed at all of them while I did all the stuff associated with my "trade." I stole from the blind; I became an alcoholic; I was addicted to drugs—I was one bad woman! Was I happy? Did I ever feel fulfilled? What do you think? I looked with envy on other Jewish wives and mothers and knew what I was missing. There was a huge hole of nothingness inside of me. And I was lonely. No woman wanted to be my friend, and no man was interested in me other than for my body.

Soon stories began floating through our community that a new rabbi, a great teacher was doing miraculous things. The stories almost seemed too good to be true. He was so different than our typical religious leaders. He loved children and took time for them. He was on the side of the poor, the sick, even the lepers, and most of all, the sinners. Some people said these were only rumors, but others believed. There was talk of lame people walking, deaf people hearing, blind people seeing, and rotten sinners being forgiven. How I longed to be set free from my current situation! I was so thirsty for help and forgiveness I could taste it.

I tried to catch him in action, but for some reason I always seemed to miss him. He always seemed to be on the move, as though he was driven to get to as many folks as possible.

Then I heard about "the" dinner invitation! One of my customers told me he was the guest of honor at this dinner given by Simon, the pompous, self-righteous Pharisee. I could tell you a dark secret thing or two about this Simon and his bunch. I hardly believed that this Jesus guy would have dinner with them. I also surmised it might have been a set-up, a dinner to disgrace the Teacher.

And I knew immediately my name wasn't on that guest list! I was scum, in Simon's mind, a nothing, a nobody, a sinner. But somehow I knew I just had to get to Jesus.

But how? It was getting late, and the first course was already underway. Quickly I grabbed my most costly thing in the house—a flask with Chanel #5. I didn't exactly know how this would work, but I knew I needed something to give the Teacher.

I managed to slip in the back gate, through the back door, and into the kitchen. I made it past the host and hostess and the guest book. They were all busy, too busy to catch me.

I made my way to the dining room; spotting the Master was not a problem. There was something magnetic about him. Something inside of me was drawn immediately to him. Even if I was dirty and he was clean.

Carefully I came up behind him, not really knowing what to do next. It was like a dam inside of me broke and all the hurt, pain, dirt, rejection, remorse, and regrets spilled out! I can't explain it!

I began weeping uncontrollably—something I hadn't done in years. My outer defensive crust had been carefully built in anger and frustration, but now it was all busted to pieces. I fell to my knees; my tears were enough to wash his dusty feet. I kissed his feet and broke open the bottle of perfume and lovingly poured it on his feet in a special anointing. My hair was the only towel handy and I began drying his feet.

The perfume wafted through the room and snapped the whole room of guests to attention! Oh, oh...now what? Jesus looked at me with compassion like no man had ever looked at me before. It was not in a sensual way, but rather in a loving God-like way. It stirred something deep in my soul.

He turned to Simon the Pharisee and said, "Simon, you and I need to have a little talk."

To which Simon replied, "Tell me."

I was now caught in the drama of this exchange. Nothing had been said to me, yet. Nobody made a move to throw me out.

The Teacher told the most incredible story, "Two men were in debt. One owed $500 and the other $50,000. Neither could pay it back. So the banker canceled both debts. Now, Simon, which of these will love him more?"

Simon was on the spot before the Teacher and his cynical guests who were curious about the man. Simon was caught; he looked around and everyone shrugged, so reluctantly he replied, "I suppose the one with the largest debt cancelation."

Jesus smiled and said, "You get the prize, you gave the correct answer."

To my dying day I will never forget what happened next. Jesus turned to me with that look of compassion but addressed Simon, "This woman came into your house. You didn't do the common courtesy of washing my feet; she washed them with her tears and wiped them dry with her hair. You didn't welcome me with the courtesy of a kiss, but she hasn't stopped kissing my feet and even poured perfume on them. Now Simon, hear this well—her many sins have been forgiven! She has been forgiven much and therefore she loves much."

Simon hadn't offered Jesus the common, everyday courtesies of a basin of water and someone to wash his feet, oil for the weary traveler, or a kiss of greeting. We all knew what Jesus meant—Simon had never asked for forgiveness because he considered himself righteous. Therefore there was little love in his life for the Lord or for others.

My life was filled to overflowing with multiple sins—I was a rank, dirty, nasty sinner, and everyone knew it. Most of all, I knew it, too, but I did not think I could ever get rid of my sins.

Jesus now spoke directly to me, loud enough for all in the room to hear it, too: "Your sins are forgiven!" Never in my life had I heard such wonderful words! My sins were forgiven. I was set free!

Immediately the buzz around the table among the other guests was: "Who is this man who forgives sins?" "The very idea!" "How can he do this?" "What right does he have to erase her past—she should pay for her sins!" Jesus took them all in with a look that silenced this chatter.

He turned back to me: "Your faith has saved you!" The joy of being forgiven began bubbling up inside of me. I was no longer the same woman! I came in a sinner, and could leave as a forgiven lady! It was a new start for me. I knew my life would be brand new from that moment on.

Jesus continued, "Go in peace!" Gone was all my guilt, and there was no disgrace to my name!

WISDOM FOR 21ST CENTURY LIVING
FROM THE LIFE OF A FORMER SINNER...

There's really a single truth that stands as tall as Mount Everest. You can never fall so low that the Master of life cannot reach down to lift you up. When you have failed, this is an opportunity for him to demonstrate his forgiveness to you as a lesson for this world.

Notice Jesus did not call Mary a "sinner." In fact, he never addressed anybody like this. He looked beyond the sin, He doesn't point fingers and tell the world how bad we really are. He extends to all of us a hand the helps and a promise of forgiveness. He takes the messed up record of our lives and gives us a whole new start—clean white pages on which we can write a new beginning. We can start over with his love and forgiveness.

Let's help those who might have fallen just as you and I have fallen and been forgiven. It's time to go in peace and live a life of gratitude!

Chapter Thirteen

BERNICE

Desperate for power and control

 This was one bad woman! And I believe she may have been proud of it. At least she flaunted her lifestyle for all the world to see. Her daddy was one nasty dude, too. He was Herod Agrippa the First, who ruled from 38 to 45 A.D. He is described as the one "who vexed the church."

Bernice first married Marcus, and then she married her uncle Herod, the one who was king of Chalcis. When he died, she married her brother Agrippa the Second. She then left Agrippa to marry Ptolemy, king of Cilicia, whom she left to go back with her brother Agrippa. Eventually she became the mistress of Vespasian and then married his son Titus when he became emperor. He got tired of her and threw her out, so she went back to her brother. Whew! What a lifestyle...just like a modern-day version of "Desperate Housewives" TV fare. Is it possible to learn anything of value from such a character? Let's hear her story and then you decide.

Scripture: *Acts 25:13, 23, 26:30*

HER SIDE OF THE STORY...

Let me be real honest at the start. If you had really known me, you would have seen me for my real self. And that's not so bad. Really, I wasn't all bad. It's just...well, you see, I had no will power, and I was a power grabber and schemer who was not about to let anything stand in my way. Yes, I went from bed to bed and man to man. But these men were all power-broker kind of guys in my world. It was pretty heady stuff. And, really, the only talent I had was the ability to seduce men, so I had to make the best of what I had before it all started to sag.

Enough...let's start at the beginning. My memory is a bit faulty and time has colored my perceptions. Any girl's story begins with her daddy. If you had known my daddy that explains lots of things. He was a great teacher! To know about my daddy you must also meet my grandpa. My daddy and my grandpappy were both named "Herod" which really was a family name...sort of like a surname. Grandpa was "Herod the Great," and all the other ruling males in our family were known as Herod, too. My daddy was "Herod Agrippa I" and other family members were Herod Archaelaus, Herod Antipas, Herod Philip II, and Herod Agrippa II. All real nice guys, that is if you didn't have to live under their rule. There were four generations of Herods, and all were in some way identified with the governments of Palestine or Israel. And all are mentioned in the New Testament of the Bible. I really think my granddad was the most ruthless of the bunch. But, for sure, not a one of these men ever won a citation for being "Nicest-Man-of-the-Year" in Palestine! I hope I haven't bored you with this dry history lesson. Please hold on, I'll get to the good stuff.

One more bit of background is important. It's about my neighborhood and culture, which gives you a more complete picture of my life. Granddad started early; he was made a king in Galilee when he was only 15 years old! How many 15-year-olds do you know who could be a real king? See what I mean.

Later he was placed on the throne of the whole area by the famous Mark Antony, who persuaded the Roman Senate to make him a real king. But in order to be a ruling king in Israel he had to conquer Jerusalem, which he did about 37 B.C.

I must deviate a bit more. You people living in a politically correct country have no possible way in which to identify with the rulers of my day. Yes, they were ruthless. Yes, they were cruel and sadistic. Yes, they were tyrants. Yes, they were really bad to the bone. Yes, they had egos so large they couldn't fit into the Roman Coliseum. Yes, they took everything and anything they wanted just because they could. Yes, they all built monuments to satisfy their egos. Yes, they were spoiled, pampered, and impossible to live with. Yes, they were all eccentric. But it sure was a hoot growing up and being part of all this fun. Of course, being the king's daughter or son had privileges, and I took advantage of every one of them. In a word, I grew up as one really, really snotty-nosed spoiled brat. In fact, I gave a whole new meaning to the type.

It didn't take me long to understand that all the spoiled ruling-class males of my day were susceptible to a pretty face and a lush, nubile body. I had it, and I used it! The history of my personal life doesn't tell the whole story by any means. I lived in a day and time when anything goes! There were no boundaries and no restraints. I was addicted to drugs (opium was the drug of choice), alcohol, clothes, sexual orgies (I guess I was what you might call a "nympho-maniac" in your day), and raw power. I was definitely what you call a control freak.

However, one vice was more important to me than any of the others—I was hooked on power! I wanted to control powerful men. I wanted people to see me in all my power and splendor. And beauty, sex and brains were my ticket to this kind of living. One more thing: You need to know I was equally as ruthless as my granddaddy. I was more subtle than he was, but nobody could stand in my way!

I really tried to live up to my name which means "victorious" or "carrying off a victory." I like the second meaning best. Life, in my eyes, was a battle or a game. I wanted to be the winner at this game of life, at any cost, even if it meant selling my soul and body to the highest bidder. I saw each of my husbands and affairs as someone or something to conquer, so I could pull off another victory. It's sort of like notches on your gun. In my day, it was notches on your sword. Only I didn't carry a sword because it would be too heavy and unladylike. So I carried a concealed stiletto, just in case. A girl really needs to look out for herself. I should also tell you I had a few people who stood in my way placed on daddy's hit-list.

My first husband was a real disaster! I should have known better. After all, I was the oldest daughter of my mom. Now she was a piece of work. She selected Marcus for me. What a weak, linguini-spined wimp he turned out to be! He was a mess. I quickly knew he wouldn't go very far in my cut-throat world, so I dumped him. My next beau was somewhat better, but he was a doddering old man who just couldn't keep up with me. He was good old Uncle Herod, king of Chalcis! He died soon after we were married, and I might have had something to do with that. I became a very rich young widow—need I say more?

My next lover was quite a hunk (or maybe I should say my next victim). You should know he was handsome even though he was my own brother! Yes, I admit it was incest, but what a kick! If you were rich and famous you could pull off this incest thing in public without tarnishing your reputation. Lots of this took place in Rome, not so much in Israel. It was fun while it lasted with Agrippa and I flaunted it. No, we never officially married, but I grew tired of him.

Next on my list to conquer was a real man of power: Ptolemy, king of Cilicia. Just to show him who was in control, I forced him to embrace Judaism and be circumcised. What a hoot! After I added him to my list, I quickly tired of him and went back to my lover-boy brother.

Soon another opportunity came to me—another famous, wealthy, and powerful king, Vespasian. Perhaps you've read about him in history. Quite a catch. But he was getting old, too. He had this stud of a son, Titus. Now here was my kind of a man: virile, young, a climber on his way to the top. It was a nice little arrangement with both father and son as my lovers. I went along for the ride. It worked for a while, but when Titus became the emperor, he no longer needed me and threw me out of his palace on my ear, telling me to never come back! That's how close I came to being queen of the whole Roman Empire and the most powerful woman in the world! How do you like that? After I'd given my all to help him climb to the top of success, he dumped me! The ungrateful swine! (I understand the same thing is still happening in your world...well, welcome to the club, sister.)

Whose bed did I end up in then? It's as though I was used up. It sure took me a lot longer in front of the mirror to get looking good. It's the pits to grow old when no one wants you anymore. Well, I decided to go back to my good old brother Agrippa. I still knew how to push his buttons to get my own way. And so I ended my days as his consort. I was always on his arm and shared in his power. You may be looking down your nose at me and my life. But, compared to Cleopatra, who really played in the big time arena, I was small peanuts.

I want to confess something I never told anybody else—my life was always meaningless and empty. I had no kids to love. I had no lasting happiness. I always needed more and more to satisfy myself. Yes, I had developed a powerful façade, but no one knew how much of an empty shell I really was. I became one sick puppy in my later years. I had some kind of "social" disease I had picked up from someone along the way. Of course, I still pretended to be happy. But you couldn't find a more miserable person in our hollow, empty society. All of us were morally bankrupt.

There is one event in my sordid life that forever links me with your Bible. It's so sad that every time I think of it, I become even more depressed. I wonder what would have happened to me and all the others I touched with my lust-filled lifestyle if that one event had ended differently.

Paul was his name—my world's leading evangelist. He drew huge crowds wherever he spoke. He was powerful, highly educated, and very persuasive. Thousands of people became Christians because of this man. Thousands were healed of all kinds of diseases. It was awesome!

Finally, the Roman Empire couldn't tolerate the movement Paul led. He and his followers were turning our world upside down! He was imprisoned, but no one knew what to do with him, so he was passed from one ruler to the next. Then, finally, it was our turn. Agrippa and I had a private audience with this guy. He preached a spell-binding message. It was as though fire burned in his belly. Then, dramatically, he made his final appeal and put the ball in our court. I looked over at my brother and lover who returned my glance with the strangest look in his eyes. I was afraid he was about to do something drastic, something foolish. I slowly shook my head "no" in his direction. He sat silently. It was almost embarrassing how long he just sat there without saying anything. Finally, Agrippa, in a voice filled with emotion said, "Paul...you have almost persuaded me to become a Christian!"

Agrippa looked at me, and I nodded in agreement. Paul was asking too much of us! Think of all we would have had to give up—our affairs, our lifestyle, and even most likely our power base! How could the Roman Empire tolerate these

Christians in leadership? We might have ended up like Paul, in one of our own dungeons. No, ma'am; no sir, not us! We both nodded in agreement; it was much too much. But it haunted me to my dying day. "Almost... almost...almost..." It became the stuff of my nightmares. I couldn't shake it. "Almost!"

Agrippa and I are forever linked to the message of your God's mercy and grace, and we refused it. From my perspective today, you don't want to be where I have been spending my years following my rejection! I look back over my completely useless life and have often wondered what kind of a different record could have been written by Bernice and Agrippa if we had become Christians and followed Jesus Christ.

CLASSIC WISDOM FOR 21ST CENTURY LIVING
FROM THE LIFE OF BERNICE...

The life lessons here are stark but simple. Bernice and her sister, Drusilla, were considered to be two of the most corrupt and shameless women of their time in Roman history. Of what value were their lives? Simply a sad example of what not to do with your life.

If hereditary stands for anything at all, these sad lessons have been forcibly taught in the history of the Herod family. History shows that not a single one of them lived an exemplary, positive lifestyle. History also records the continual downward spiral of their sinful, sordid lifestyle. I can't find one redeeming value from this family.

Perhaps there's a lesson for our nation to be found in the fall of the ancient Roman Empire. Much of our democracy is based on some of the same principles which made the Romans strong. But today, we see the same cracks in the foundations upon which they, as well as we, were built. How much longer will our society last if we continue down the slippery slope of moral decline that we are observing and tolerating today?

Chapter Fourteen

THE SYRO-PHOENICIAN WOMAN

Desperate for her daughter's deliverance

 This is one remarkable female...nameless, yes, and called "a woman from Canaan," by Matthew, but called "a Greek" by the writer Mark. There's no contradiction—these terms were used to show the difference of a Gentile from a Jew. She was considered a "heathen" by the Jews. We know nothing more of her other than she was a very concerned mother.

The Bible is full of stories of "demon possession." It's mentioned more than 70 times in the New Testament but only twice in the Old Testament. Demons are fallen angels under the direction of the devil, Satan. People are not "devil" possessed, they are "demon" possessed. The demons' only goal is to place people in bondage and thwart the plan of God. If they can possess people, so much the better for their plans. Note, however, demons and the devil are not more powerful than Jesus Christ, and they recognize him as God's son. Whenever these minions of hell came face to face with Christ or his disciples, they trembled and always did his bidding!

Scripture: *Matthew 15:21-28; Mark 7:24-30*

HER SIDE OF THE STORY...

Her little body jerked, twisted, and convulsed with thrashing arms and legs. With eyes wide open, our little girl mumbled to beings I could not see nor sense. When these episodes happened, without warning, her face was contorted in fear and pain. Her voice changed, and there was a weird kind of high pitched laughing that was not laughing. I couldn't get through to her. She perspired profusely as though she were having a strenuous workout. My husband and I had the most helpless feeling. There was nothing we could do other than wait out these tortuous spells.

It was as though somebody had stolen our daughter from us—both body and soul. After these spells were over, she was exhausted and fell into a deep sleep. What was happening to our only child? There were no more hugs, no more soft kisses. My husband and I hardly dared fall asleep at night for fear of an attack that might take her from us. We lived with this constant possibility. Our doctors were helpless. Her diagnosis was that she was "demon possessed." It was a kind of catch all phrase for anything we didn't understand. We were desperate. We were willing to give everything we had if only she could be helped. Our family life was quickly spiraling downward. Our every waking thoughts and concerns were about our little girl, her safety, and her future. We were puzzled by this ever darkening problem. How had it happened? How did this innocent one open herself up to such a vile bondage? We searched our minds and our past. How? When? And most importantly, is there a cure? Is there an answer for her and for us?

Then stories and rumors began to filter into our area about a healer, a teacher who was Jewish. We heard that he healed people of various ailments, but most fascinating to my husband and me were the persistent stories about his ability to heal people of demon possession. But how were we ever going to be near enough to him to bring our daughter to him for—dare I even think about it—a healing? Travel with her was just about impossible.

We first heard about him walking on water! Now how wonderful is that? Then we heard about how he had fed a hungry crowd of more than 20,000 people, kids included, with fish and bread. But most exciting to us was the report of healing a man filled with a legion of demons. Our little daughter had only one demon so surely this teacher could heal her. I believed he could! I really became a believer in this man and his power. My husband had his doubts, but I was desperate for some hope. I knew in my heart this man was the only answer for our little Rebekah.

Then word got out that the Master was on his way for a few days of rest in our area of Tyre and Sidon. It was unusual that a Jew would spend time with us Gentiles. We were led to understand he was doing this to get away from the crowds that thronged him and his followers. I promised myself that I would do whatever it took to get to this man for his help. If I had to crawl on broken shards, I would do it. I was really desperate because her condition kept on getting worse and worse.

He came to a secret hide-away just outside of Tyre, but how could anybody keep his presence a secret? I did my own investigation until I figured out which house it was. I knew I had to go alone because my husband had to stay with our daughter. I walked right through the door, but I wasn't sure, at first, how to address him to get his attention.

With all the chutzpah I could muster, I just plunged in and cried out: "Lord, Son of David have mercy on me! My little daughter is suffering terribly from being demon possessed." He ignored me, maybe because I was a woman and a Gentile at that. Yes, I did stand out in this crowd. I sure didn't dress like these peasants who followed him. I decided to talk to his disciples until I got some kind of a response. (I never give up easily.) First it was Peter, then James, and John, and all the rest. "Help me, please!" "Listen to me..." "It's my daughter!" Finally I pestered them long enough and loud enough that they finally got Jesus' attention.

"Please send this woman away," they cried to him. "She keeps crying to us about her daughter. We can't take it anymore. Do something!"

He calmly replied, "Tell her I was sent only to the Jewish people, not to Phoenicians." He spoke to his disciples, not to me, but I overheard. Now was the time to take really drastic measures. I refused to accept this brush-off for my daughter!

I threw myself at his feet, "Lord, help me!" Maybe my crying would do some good, too.

He carefully explained, "I was sent only to the Jewish people." And for the first time he looked at me and then went on, "It's not right for me to take their bread and toss it under the table to the family dogs."

I was not going to let that deter me either! I was there with a purpose. I needed this man's help, no matter what.

I answered, "Yes, Lord, but even little dogs eat the crumbs that fall from their master's tables." Finally, I thought I had gotten through. My persistence had paid off.

He said: "O woman, you have great faith!" I knew he was pleased, but I was breathless, eagerly waiting in this pause. He continued, "Your request is answered!"

Never have words sounded so wonderful! I was ecstatic with joy! Could it really be? I didn't know whether to hug him or start shouting, so I just knelt and gave Him my praise and thanks! Then I jumped up and hugged the nearest person— who happened to be Peter—who got all flustered and didn't know what to do with a blubbering, tearful, happy mother. He finally extracted himself from my hug and off I went toward home as fast as I could to see if it were really true! Could my daughter really be healed? It was too much!

As soon as I got home, my husband met me with a joyful hug. "She's well! She's healed!" he cried. And she came running with arms wide open to give her mother a long overdue hug. We three jumped for joy, danced together, hugged and kissed and cried for happiness. Never in all my life had I been so happy! It was incredible.

Finally, when things calmed down a little bit, I asked my husband, "When did this happen?"

He said, "It was exactly mid-afternoon. She was in the middle of one of her bad seizures, and it stopped instantly. She sat up and said, 'Daddy, I'm feeling wonderful. Please get me a drink!'"

I jumped in, "That had to be around the time when tea was being served to the Master and his men. It was just after that he promised, 'Your request is granted.'"

Well you can imagine the joy and happiness of that evening and beyond. We talked and talked about the teacher and his power and his teachings and decided that we Gentiles would follow him, too.

I never quite understood why Jesus gave me such a rough time, but as I think back, I'm sure it was a test of my faith. Yes, a test of my faith. I'm glad to tell you, I didn't give up, and you shouldn't either.

WISDOM FOR 21ST CENTURY LIVING
FROM ANOTHER NAMELESS WOMAN FROM TYRE...

What can a pagan woman teach us sophisticated people of the enlightened 21st century? Well, quite a bit when we stop to think about it.

First, if she had not heard about the Christ there would have been no cure for her demon-possessed daughter. Evil and evil spirits are not only problems of a by-gone era. We, too, are in a battle with all kinds of evil in our day. The answer for help and deliverance is also found today in a relationship with Jesus.

Second, faith is not only expressed in words, it is also expressed in meaningful actions. This woman put her faith into action. She pursued Jesus and his disciples until the Master met the needs she was expressing. She never gave up.

Third, we have a responsibility to build a hedge of prayer about our kids and others we love. In faith, believe every member of your family is surrounded and protected by a loving God as you place them in His care and keeping. It's not the time to worry; it's the time to pray and believe for their protection.

Fourth, remember, Jesus Christ and his power to deliver and heal is the same today as it was yesterday. Therefore, we may need to be more persistent in our faith and in our praying. We should never give up!

Chapter Fifteen

LOIS...THE BIBLE'S ONLY GRANDMA

Desperate to pass along her faith

 Of course there are lots of grandmothers mentioned in the Bible, but Lois is the only one given the designation "grandmother." The term is used only once in the Bible and Lois is it!

Hers is an old Greek name meaning "agreeable or desirable." What an appropriate name for a godly grandmother! We don't know much about her other than she was a devout Jewess who passed her devotion to her daughter, Eunice, and on to her grandson, Timothy. Along with family members she lived in Lystra. It's highly possible this family were converts under the Apostle Paul's ministry, and we also assume he may have been a guest more than once in their home. Interesting, there is no mention of Timothy's father or grandfather. All we know of his father is that he was a Gentile, which may or may not have been a problem in this marriage. Paul commended only the faith of the grandmother and mother.

Scripture: *II Timothy 1:5; Acts 14:6-7; 16:1*

HER SIDE OF THE STORY...

I am so proud to be the only grandmother named as such in the Bible. What an honor! I really didn't find out about this until after I was dead and gone when the Apostle wrote his letter to my grandson.

I was a typical Jewish grandmother with a handy cookie jar, bragging rights on my kids and grandson, lots of hugs and kisses, a warm bosom for little ones to be cradled on, a full knitting basket, special grandmotherly recipes, and a highly defined sense of humor.

Being a grandmother was a highlight of my life. It was so much fun I think I should have had only grandkids. Not only was I grandma to little Timmy but to all his friends, too. My house was a favorite place for other kids too. This being a grandmother is the greatest assignment in the world.

However, I must tell you that my daughter Eunice, against my better judgment, got mixed up in an unfortunate marriage. She went outside the Jewish faith and married a Gentile man. Everything was a problem between them because our culture was centered around the Torah and the Temple. He didn't abuse or beat her, but it just wasn't working out very well. I worried and prayed about it. I even suggested marriage counseling. He simply refused to have anything to do with our faith. It really came to a head after little Timmy was born.

Eunice insisted he be brought to the Temple when he was eight days old for his circumcision and dedication. Her husband really threw a fit and threatened all sorts of dire consequences if this was done. Poor Timmy—he was a misfit with his Gentile relatives and a half outcast with our Jewish family. You could cut the tension with a knife at times.It was not good.

The final straw happened when Timmy was old enough to go to school. Eunice insisted on his going to the synagogue school for a proper Jewish education, but his father said, "No. He will be educated in one of our Greek schools, a public school!" And the battle raged—one thing led to another and this broken home finally ended in a nasty divorce.

Eunice and Timothy were thrown out by their Gentile father and forced to move in with me. You know, grandmothers see a whole lot of things, but don't say much. She and little Timmy were broken. Poor little boy, he didn't understand why this had to happen. His daddy just abandoned him, and he was left to grow up with no positive male influence in his life. I did everything I could to make up for some of his loss, but there's only so much a grandma can do.

Eunice was a mess and needed my help to recover. A mother is a mother forever. But life did go on, and things got better. My humble home proved to be just what both of them needed to heal.

I grieved for Timmy's lack of a father's guidance and model in his life. Our favorite time of day was just after the evening meal. He would crawl up in my lap, and I would tell him stories about his maternal ancestors. He asked for some of them to be told over and over—especially Abraham, Isaac, and Jacob. He wanted to know how our people came out of the bondage of Egypt, how they crossed the Red Sea on dry ground, and how Moses brought the Ten Commandments down from the mountain.

He especially loved to hear about Samson and his feats of strength, David and the killing of Goliath, and Elijah and the chariots taking him away. I loved to whisper in his ears the stories of the three fire-proof guys: Daniel shutting the mouths of lions, Ezekiel and his wheel in the middle of the wheels, and Jonah in the mouth of the big fish. He loved them all.

I did everything I could to give him a good Jewish educational background. He memorized the Torah like all good

Jewish boys. But I was so sorry he was excluded from all the kids programs at our local synagogue. They refused him because "he wasn't circumcised." Why take it out on a little innocent boy? I never did understand. Weren't we supposed to make converts? It sure didn't happen at our synagogue.

We had been hearing persistent rumors about the young, vibrant Messiah—his miraculous birth, his ministry of healings and miracles, his teachings, his untimely death, and his unbelievable miraculous return from death. We became aware of his followers who were spreading out through our land and preaching a "gospel" of good news. Yes, we were curious. Yes, I was spiritually hungry for more of God. Our system was so sterile and unsatisfying. In fact, between you and me, it was also boring—there was no life to it. I left every meeting with a hunger for something more.

Then, we heard that the world renowned evangelist named Paul was coming to our town to hold meetings. I was really excited and curious. I wanted to hear about this exciting Messiah and this new thing called a "church." We knew about synagogues and temples, but what was a church?

The day came. Eunice was a bit reluctant, but I insisted that she and Timothy come along with me to the meeting. When we arrived, it seemed as though the whole town was there. There was happy, wonderful singing and worship, and then Paul began preaching. Never in my life had I ever heard such things. Never had anybody spoken with such clarity; there was no beating around the bush. I loved it! He was a powerful, persuasive preacher. The crowd hung on his every word.

He ended with an invitation for all who wanted to follow Jesus Christ, the only Son of God who had come to redeem all of us from our sins. I was always taught that the blood of bulls and goats was atonement enough. But no, Paul said there was a new and a living way through Jesus Christ and our faith in his sacrifice on the cross. I believed! I accepted Jesus as my personal Savior and promised to live the rest of my life for him! I looked over at Eunice; she was weeping and, for the first time in a long time, she was praying. Timothy also accepted in faith the Messiah into his life. This experience changed our lives forever!

We met the apostle in person and what a man! Being the grandmother, I invited him to our home for a specially cooked meal, and he accepted! Later I found out, I was the only who thought about such mundane things as feeding a hungry man.

As I was preparing the evening meal, I couldn't help but notice that Paul took a real liking to Timothy and Timothy to him. I was thrilled when this dynamic preacher eventually addressed Timothy as "my son." I got goose bumps all over me. I was so excited I thought my heart would burst out of my chest.

Paul the apostle of Jesus Christ, in my home, reaching out to my Timothy. I just knew in my spirit this was the male mentor he needed in his life. That was the beginning. I could not have asked for more. I just knew that Paul sensed something very special in my grandson.

The apostle left and went on his way, but he returned many times to our home. The relationship between Paul and Timothy progressed, and soon Timothy became involved in ministry. He became part of our church, which Paul had founded in Thessalonica. Soon he was traveling with Paul on some of his journeys. What a team they made—Paul, Silas, and Timothy! I was so proud and excited about the wonderful young witness for the Lord that Timothy had become. And Paul always addressed him as "my true son" or simply "my son."

Much later after Timothy had matured, he became one of the major leaders in our churches. Sadly, Paul was captured and held in prison. But word kept filtering back to us about how many of those prison guards became believers when they were chained to Paul for four-hour shifts at a time. I can just imagine the conversations—these guys were more like captives than Paul who turned the tables on them. This was so powerful that Christianity began permeating into Caesar's household! Imagine! I chuckled inside and thought, *That's the apostle at work...go for it, Paul!* He never missed the opportunity to tell others about our Lord, and now Timothy was doing the same thing.

Paul, bless his heart, wrote two of the most powerful and helpful letters to my grandson. He addressed them, "To Timothy, my dear son." These two letters were filled with encouragement, warnings, challenges, and teachings. The letters became read far and wide and eventually became part of the New Testament.

Of course I didn't do all of this for Timothy in order to have Paul give me a mention in his second letter. However, I gladly accepted it when Paul said, "Timothy, you've known the Bible all your life because you began way back on your grandma's knee." That was my plan from the beginning of Timothy's life—I wanted him to know all there was to know about God.

WISDOM FOR 21ST CENTURY LIVING
FROM THE LIFE OF A GODLY GRANDMOTHER...

Every child needs a grandparent who can pass along the faith to them, especially when the child is young. Grandmothers have more time to be patient with young ones. Each child needs a mentor, an example, a role model to follow. Too often moms and dads are so busy earning a living they have no quality time with their kids—not on purpose, mind you, but they are just too busy working two jobs and attending

PTA, sports, and ballet lessons, and overseeing homework.

Many of you know of grandparents who walk into church Sunday after Sunday with a grandchild who has been "spiritually" orphaned. Parents sometimes don't take time for church. So be the grandparent who is willing to bridge the gap. One of the greatest gifts that a grandparent can give is the life-long advantage of knowing God.

Never give up on a grandchild! If need be, become the child's spiritual mentor. The time you spend with your grandchildren is never wasted!

Chapter Sixteen

SAPPHIRA

Desperate to appear generous

Her name, "Sapphira" really means the precious gemstone, "sapphire." Likely she was named this because it would match the deep blue of her eyes. The name also comes from a Hebrew word signifying "beautiful" or "pleasant."

Beyond her name or her husband's name, the Bible gives us nothing more—no genealogy, no other family information, nothing except what we can infer. Likely they were members of the First Church, but they could have been true believers or hypocrites. We do know about their greed and deceit.

Scripture: *Acts 5:1-11*

HER SIDE OF THE STORY...

A whole lot of people think of me as having been led astray by my greed and the greed of my husband.

In reality, Ananias, my partner-in-crime, was easily led. I had easily wrapped him around my little finger. Poor dear, he never knew what hit him or how he had been used by me. Really, I wasn't a bad person. I was generous, almost to a fault. We were respectable church members, even part of the leadership team at First Church. Just between you and me, I will confess to a weakness: I always wanted to impress people with my importance. That's all. Just one deadly weakness was my downfall.

I won't waste your time with my background, but I'll get right to the point of this story and why my name is so memorable. Our beloved First Church was the most exciting, wonderful new thing in the entire history of our city. It was fabulous, and our growth was out of sight! Ananias and I were charter members. When you see a good thing like this, you need to jump right in, help it grow, and work your way to the inside of things. I tell you, you've never seen anything like this in history! Everybody was filled with awe at the miraculous happenings. We had all left our formal, ritualistic Judaism to embrace this new movement called Christianity. It came together on Pentecost when, in one day, 3,000 members were added to the original followers of the rabbi called Jesus. We were two of the original 3,000!

The fellowship was something else! We shared everything, including our meals, with each other and especially with those who were not so fortunate. The joy of giving was incredible: Widows and single-parent families were helped; the elderly were cared for; children were well-fed and clothed. It was the greatest social experiment we had ever seen. We shared with each other both in our homes and in the temple courts. We were pioneering something that had never been done before. We were breaking new ground, and we all loved it! It was something new both in human relationships and in our worship of the Lord.

Those days were the high point of a voluntary Christian community in the emerging church. There was no compulsory law to do what we were doing. People willingly gave everything from the sales of their homes and properties. It was not like the godless communism of your own time where people are forced into an "equal" distribution of goods and property, and human rights are trampled. No, ours was for the sake of Jesus Christ and His Church. There was a pureness and wholeness about this unselfish willingness to share, caused by the new birth of the followers of this rabbi and his teachings.

One day, as we were gathered in worship, Barney, the man we all called "The Son of Encouragement," sold his farm and placed the money in the offering plate at the feet of the apostles. Immediately there was a great outburst of praise for this unselfish, sacrificial gift! The apostles gave Barney huge hugs! It was quite a scene for this humble man and his gift.

I punched Ananias in the ribs as I sidled close to him and whispered over the din, "Why don't we do the same thing?" Maybe my motives were not as pure as Barney's because something inside of me longed to be noticed. Where did such thoughts come from? My pride? Or was it the devil at work in me, doing a job on my head and heart? I guess you'll have to decide.

We left the meeting that day and immediately got in touch with our real estate broker. We gave him directions to sell a piece of our property. It was soon appraised and the price set. Within the week we had a buyer—a developer who knew of plans to build an arena on that site. (He had an inside track because he had bribed someone.) So in order to keep things quiet and so we wouldn't complain later, he gave us double our asking price! He paid us the asking price, which would be a matter of public information for all to see, and under the table, he paid us more to keep us quiet.

We had this wonderful windfall nobody knew about! I looked at my spineless husband, grinning from ear to ear. He said, "What?" He must have seen that gleam in my eye and knew my thoughts were on how quickly I could get to the shops before they closed that day. "Okay...okay," he said, "Go to it, baby."

Honey...those words are like saying sic 'em to a dog. What a day in the market I had! Ananias didn't let any grass grow under his feet either! He beat a path down to the local camel trader and brought home some fine specimens for our next vacation.

I almost forgot to tell you—we didn't have any kids, so we could spend our windfall on just the two of us. (Kids would have slowed down our lifestyle.)

Over our dinner that night, we planned our special presentation to the apostles in front of the whole church two days later. I suggested, "Ananias, love, nobody knows about our windfall. But the purchase price will be public knowledge. Let's agree that, when we give the money, we say this is the whole amount we received for the property. The folks will think it's great that we, like Barney, gave our all. They'll love us!"

He looked at me and raised his eyebrows. "Are you sure, honey? That's not kosher. I'm really not sure we should do that."

"Look, they will all know the selling price, but nobody knows about the rest. If we agree on the same story, it'll work. Believe me, no one will know differently. Okay?"

Reluctantly he agreed. "Alright, but how will we pull this off?"

"You go to the first service with cash. That will really impress them; then I'll come for the second service, and we'll get twice the mileage out of our gift. Okay? Yes, that will work!" Finally my husband was convinced.

Sunday morning came and when Ananias was getting dressed, I told him, "Don't put on anything new. We shouldn't over do it. We need to play down our personal appearance since we weren't supposed to have gotten anything out of the sale. And, whatever you do, don't take the new camel." Good advice if I must say so, myself.

Ananias started for the door, and I ran to give him a kiss for good luck. I made sure the bag of cash was in his hand and said, "Honey, remember our little story, and you'll be a hero today!"

I didn't find out until too late about the events that happened. When offering time came in the service, the plates were passed. At the appropriate time, when all eyes were focused on Peter, Ananias made his triumphal saunter to the front. And with a dramatic gesture, he laid the cash at Peter's feet and stood up to the intoxicating sound of applause and praise.

Ananias announced, "We sold it for this much, and we are giving it all to the church."

At this Peter signaled for silence, and people pressed forward, wondering what was happening.

Peter looked Ananias square in the eyes and asked, "Ananias, how is it possible that Satan has enticed you to lie to the Holy Spirit and hold back some for yourself?"

Peter continued, "Why? It was your money and land before you sold it. It was yours after you sold it. But you kept back part of it and now pretend you have given it all. You have lied to God!" Peter thundered the last line so everyone could hear.

When my husband heard this, he collapsed in a heap and was dead before he hit the floor. Talk about a dramatic scene in church! You don't see this every Sunday, and people fell on their faces in fear before God.

Well…none of my friends came looking for me to warn me me or tell me what had happened. I was at the market doing more shopping, but I watched my time and about three hours later when the second service would be starting, I made my way to the Temple.

This was to be my shining hour. Ananias and I would be given the same honored status as Barney. Shivers of anticipation played up and down my spine. When I made my dramatic entrance, I didn't even notice that nobody was smiling. If I had been more aware of what was going on, I would have noticed that the place was like the inside of a tomb.

I made my way to the front row so everybody would notice me. I was sure they would be thinking that my husband and I were better than anybody else because of our wonderful, sacrificial gift to benefit the church. It would place us in line for the next level of leadership.

Peter motioned for me to step forward and join him on the platform. Yes! What a moment! For the whole congregation to see me at my best. Peter looked at me with a sad expression and held up the sack of cash for all to see again and asked, "Sapphira, tell me, is this the price you and Ananias got for the land?"

"Yes...that is the price." I knew it was a blatant, bold-faced lie, but in my greed and desire for recognition and applause, it was a small price to pay. I looked at Peter again—he certainly didn't look impressed.

Then he said, "How could you agree with your husband to lie and test the Spirit of the Lord?" I instantly began to get light-headed and thought I was about to faint.

"Look!" And Peter pointed to the ushers. "Here are the men who just dragged your dead husband out of the Temple and buried him. They will now take your dead body out the door and bury you alongside!" Those were the very last words I heard uttered on earth. I fell over, and before I hit the floor, I was dead. I can't believe how quickly it happened. I was taking a breath one second and dead the next.

They dragged me out and buried me with my husband. We had no family or friends to even mourn our passing. Everyone was scared to death to even come near our poor, dead bodies.

At my death, the account says, "Great fear seized the whole church and everybody else who heard about these events!"

WISDOM FOR 21ST CENTURY LIVING
FROM THE LIFE OF SAPPHIRA...

What an absolutely incredible story! Just think of how many vacant pews our churches would have today if every one who lied to the Holy Spirit or God would be struck dead! Perhaps a healthy fear is what is needed to spark a real renewal and revival in our dead churches!

The Bible is perfectly clear in the fact that God delights in us when we give simply for the joy of giving. But when we give with the expectations of receiving accolades or our name engraved on brass plaques or in stone for the world to see, the joy is gone! We lost it in our hunger for approval. Learn to give when nobody is looking.

Sapphira could still have saved her life if she had just spoken the truth. Life gets very ugly when we cover up our deceits. Honesty is the only policy to live by!

Sapphira made the wrong choices because she was seeking something temporal and fleeting. She wanted something in return for her giving. If we can give and desire nothing in return, we will experience much joy.

Chapter Seventeen

THE WOMAN WHO TOUCHED JESUS

Desperate to be healed

This sick, anonymous, faith-filled woman must have been emaciated, anemic, even jaundiced. She apparently lived in the vicinity of Caesarea Philippi. She would have been declared "unclean" according to Leviticus 15:25, "When a woman has a discharge of blood for many days at a time other than her monthly period, she will be unclean as long as she has the discharge." It was almost as bad as a death sentence or the ostracism experienced by a leper.

The early church named this woman Veronica, a beautiful name. Legend also has it that she followed Christ on his painful trip to the cross and followed alongside to wipe his forehead dripping with sweat and blood. Such cloths are called "Veronicas." To our day, some churches celebrate her with a "Saint Veronica Feast Day" every July 12.

Scripture: *Matthew 9:20-22; Mark 5:25-34; Luke 8:43-48*

HER SIDE OF THE STORY...

"Unclean...unclean!" I shouted as I made my way in public. I had been declared unclean by the priest and my husband because for the last 12 years I had had a discharge of blood that never stopped. It was a serious medical condition with no known cure.

When it had begun, we had some considerable money, so my husband and I attempted to conceal my condition and went to doctors and specialists for help. Not a one could find a cure. All they did was take our hard-earned money. One of the doctors told the priest, and the priest called us to the temple grounds where he pronounced me unclean. It was more than my husband could take—it was impossible to live with an unclean wife. I didn't blame him. He left me some money and when that was used up by more doctors, I had nothing left. Fortunately, he felt sorry enough for me to give me a very small stipend, enough to eke out a humble existence.

I suspect you haven't caught on to what it meant in my day to be pronounced "unclean." It was to be unwanted and unwelcomed everywhere and by everybody, including family. My body was considered unclean. The bed I slept on was unclean. The furniture I sat on was considered unclean. The people I touched would also be unclean. If they touched me or anything I had touched or used, they became unclean, too. Then by the Mosiac law they had to wash their clothes and take a special cleansing bath and would be considered unclean until past sundown which is the start of the next day.

To be unclean for 12 long years meant...

A dozen years of never being touched by another!

A dozen years of nobody dropping by for a cup of coffee!

A dozen years of not appearing at a public function!

A dozen years of being absent from Temple worship!

A dozen years of no husband, kids, or family visiting!

A dozen years of existence as an outcast of society!

What else was considered to be "unclean" in my day? Demons and evil spirits were pronounced "unclean spirits."

You can only begin to imagine what nice people called me. It was a struggle to keep a semblance of good mental health. Isolation tore at my soul. How I yearned to be accepted, to even shake another person's hand, to be hugged by another human being, and to be kissed by one of my kids.

Think of it—4,380 days of non-stop hemorrhaging. Before this happened I was considered to be a beautiful young woman. In fact, a very desirable, happy, joyful, normal young lady. Men vied for my hand in marriage. In fact, my dad had quite a few suitors come calling and asking him for my hand in marriage. But all that changed. Now my life was filled with sadness, darkness, self-loathing, loneliness, sickness, and hopelessness. In fact, I placed my life as being a minus one on a scale of one to ten, with ten being best. My self-esteem was lower than low. What a way to live out my life! I wished many times I were dead.

I kept hearing these rumors about a man named Jesus. He was always with the sick, the lame, the blind, the outcasts, the sinners, and even the demon possessed people. And most important to me were the stories of how he reached out and touched people—even lepers, outcasts, and women! He even talked to women in public—something strictly forbidden for religious leaders to do in my day. A tiny spark of hope began to burn deep down inside. Dare I think that maybe he could help me, an unclean woman? Something awakened inside. I had to get to him, but how?

Distance was a problem for me. I lived in Caesarea Philippi, and I heard he was supposed to come to Capernaum. I had no donkey, no chariot, and no money to get between those two towns. I could only pick 'em up and put 'em down for about 30 miles! It was a two-day walk even for healthy people, but for me in my weakened and critically ill situation, it was at least a three days walk.

I was desperate. I just knew he would heal me if I could get to touch even the hem of his cloak. I just knew it. I had faith. It had to happen, but I had to hurry to catch him before he left the area.

I started early in the morning with a meager lunch. I was too weak to carry a sleeping bag so I used a shawl. There was no money for a room, so I slept by the road. It was cold and hard. There were thieves, but if they came close, I had the best secret weapon: I simply shouted, "Unclean!" Not a one of them dared come close enough to do me harm. I guess there was somewhat of a silver lining in my sordid condition.

The bleeding never stopped...what a chore. I would do my best to secretly change, and was up and walking again, early in the morning.

It was a long walk, but I began to experience hope building with each step. My feet began to bleed from the tiny, sharp stones that lodged in my sandals. I was thirsty, exhausted, and just about at the end of my strength when I painfully made my way through the streets of Capernaum. It didn't take me long to find this Jesus. It seems that everyone was running to catch a glimpse of him and see him heal somebody. The streets were thronged. I rested on a low stone wall to catch my breath and recover some bit of strength before I plunged into the crowd.

Yes, the time had come. Getting through the crowd was no big deal. I just kept saying, "Coming through...unclean, un-clean...coming through." They parted, amazing that I would dare press through the crowd.

Then I thought I saw him, the man in the middle of the crowd. Could it be? He was facing away from me. I decided that I had to get to him before he moved on. No wait, I was so close I could hear the pleading of a man, and someone whispered, "That's Jarius, the ruler in our synagogue. What is it he wants? I can't believe that he's coming to Jesus."

I saw it all and heard it all. Jarius fell at the feet of Jesus and he pleaded, with tears choking his words, "Jesus, will you please come with me to my house? My 12-year-old daughter is dying!"

Jesus gave a hand to lift Jarius up, and the two started in the direction of his home. Oh no! Quickly, I decided to make my move before he disappeared! He was walking away from me. Frantically I thought that it was either now or never. I couldn't give up even though I knew that even touching his clothes was breaking the sacred Jewish laws of cleanliness.

I lunged through the crowd immediately around Jesus and managed to fall on my knees and just barely touched the bottom fringe of his cloak!

Something wonderful happened in my body! Immediately my bleeding had stopped. I knew that all I needed was a slight touch of his robe.

Imagine that for 12 agonizing years I had never touched anybody, and no one had touched me. But somehow, in my faith I touched Jesus! That's all I needed—just a touch of faith.

Jesus stopped his walk! Oh...oh. Now what? "Who touched me?" he asked as he turned around to look. I almost laughed—everyone gave him that blank "Whooo...me" kind of look and shrugged their shoulders.

Peter jumped in, "Lord, the people are crushing you and us and you ask 'Who touched me?' Look, they're all touching you!"

But Jesus knew something special had happened; a healing energy had been discharged from him to me!

"Someone touched me in faith...I know that the power to heal has gone out from me!" And he looked right at me.

Everybody looked where he looked...yes, I stood out in this crowd, and there was no place to hide. I was dirty, dressed in the clothing of a beggar, my face was dusty, and my tears of joy were making rivulets down my cheeks. I had to tell him.

I stepped up to him and fell at his feet. There before all those prim and proper people, I told him the story about my condition. I told him how all those medical charlatans had taken everything I had. I told him why I had touched him and how grateful I was that I was instantly healed.

All the while he was looking at me with the most compassionate eyes. Then he reached for my hands and helped me stand upright.

"Daughter," he said, just like I was part of his family, "your faith has healed you! You are no longer unclean! Go in peace."

I went immediately and changed into clothes I had prepared and cleaned just for this occasion because I knew what would happen. Then, I followed him. In fact I followed him and shared my story to all who wanted to hear it.

I even followed him up the walk to the place of his crucifixion. It was horrible. All I could manage to do to be of help to him who had helped me was to periodically wipe the blood and sweat from his brow and his face. It was agonizing to see him have to suffer—the one who had been so compassionate, loving, and kind to people like me.

And I am so glad to report to you that it didn't end with his death. The news of his resurrection went through Jerusalem like an electric shock. His story just went on and on and on. I'm so thrilled to have been a part of his story...me, the unclean woman, the bleeding woman, became "The woman who, in faith, touched Jesus."

WISDOM FOR 21ST CENTURY LIVING
FROM THE WOMAN WHO TOUCHED JESUS...

If you happen to be one of those people who are close to losing hope, don't give up! I can tell you from my personal experience that God, in the person of his Son, sees your hurts, your pains, your sorrows, your needs, your seemingly impossible situation! But more than seeing, He is a God of healing, hope, help, and restoration.

When you are ready for God, when you are ready to reach out in faith, even to touch the fringe of his cloak, God is more than ready. I was ready! It works! Your faith can make a difference when you touch God in your need!

Whatever you do, never give up! Fan the faint spark of belief until it becomes a roaring fire of living faith. Help, healing, and deliverance is for you in the person and power of Jesus Christ.

Chapter Eighteen

PRISCILLA

Desperate to serve

Her name means "worthy or venerable." It's a Roman name and indicates she likely belonged to a distinguished family.

She and her husband Aquila were born in Pontus, both being Jews of Asia-Minor. They were also expelled by Claudius from Rome and settled in Corinth. They were quite a team and are always mentioned together. Three times her name is first and three times his name appears first. This couple became, in my opinion, the most important family to the Apostle Paul in his ministry. They had a prosperous tent-making business and lived well.

Scripture: *Acts 18-19; Romans 16:3-4; I Corinthians 16:19; II Timothy 4:19*

HER SIDE OF THE STORY...

It sure was great to have Paul back in our home. So much excitement was building in the many churches Paul had established. Ephesus especially was on fire, and the newly planted church was growing at a fabulous rate. Everywhere Paul went, the gospel was spreading, and multitudes became Christians. Spectacular reports came to us that even handkerchiefs taken from Paul had been used in healing many people of their sickness and others were set free from demon spirits. What a wonderful time to be alive and a part of this new, wonderful church.

Aquila and I couldn't stop laughing when we heard the story of Sceva, a Jewish exorcist, and his seven boys, who attempted to do the same thing as Paul in driving out demon spirits. They even used Paul's prayer: "In the name of Jesus, whom Paul preaches, I command you to come out!" Did it work? Ha!

The man in whom the demon had taken residence sarcastically replied to them, in fact mocking them, "Jesus I know and I know all about Paul, but who are you?"

This demon possessed man beat up all seven of these guys. They ran out of the house stark naked and bleeding from their wounds. It must have been quite a sight.

Other so-called exorcists, sorcerers, and witches put on quite a show with a public bonfire to burn up all the scrolls. All their magic potions, formulas, and incantations were worthless when exposed to the highest power of Jesus Christ as demonstrated through the life and ministry of Paul.

At this time, Ephesus was a hot-bed of idolatry and sensual idol worship. In fact, Ephesus was the home of the huge statue of Artemis, the many-breasted goddess of sensuality. We knew a riot was in the making when silversmiths took to the streets protesting Paul's evangelistic efforts. Because of Paul's evangelism and the many people who had become Christians, the silversmith business was hurting. These guys had previously earned a good living by making miniature images of Artemis.

Their spokesperson's battle cry went something like this: "Men, we are living well, but this Paul has hurt our business with his campaigns that convince people there is only one god to serve, Jesus Christ! It's a problem in all of Asia-Minor, and we've got to put a stop to this guy." There was rioting in the streets, and they even captured two of the men with Paul. And, you know Paul, he was ready to take on this crowd himself. But calmer heads prevailed, and we managed to whisk him away before they would have killed him.

Paul got the message that it was too hot to stay in this town. He left on another trip to evangelize in Macedonia. But, I've gotten ahead of my story. Let me back up a bit.

Life was good—Aquila and I were both born in Pontus and met in Rome. We had a romantic courtship, and our marriage was wonderful. We knew we were meant for each other. We thought alike, had the same interests, and went into the tent-making business together. Soon our little company grew, and, as a result, we enjoyed prosperity. The network I was born into probably helped us too. This idyllic, wonderful, peaceful life was changed when we met Paul.

Through him we became avid followers of Jesus Christ. It wasn't long before Caesar threw us Christians out of his city and confiscated our businesses. We weren't sure at first where to go. We finally traveled to the city of Corinth, another heathen stronghold, and set up shop again.

We had been a good Jewish couple, well-versed in the Torah and the prophets. But when we met Paul and he introduced us to the Messiah, we really began to live. We became avid students of the teachings of Paul. He was brilliant, educated, and an incredible mentor and teacher.

He came to Corinth to help us in our business as well as to share the gospel with the Corinthians. In fact he stayed for 18 months in our home. What a time! He was a hard worker and highly skilled in our trade. (You see, it was a point of honor that each Jewish boy learn a trade along with receiving their education.) Paul used his trade to support himself when necessary. He sure was one fine tentmaker! As we worked together planning, marketing, cutting, and sewing the tent material,

Paul was teaching us the deeper truths of the gospel of Jesus. He took us into a greater understanding of the death and resurrection of Jesus. I could listen to him all day. What a wonderful 18 months!

As was his custom, everywhere he went, Paul preached and taught and debated. He began in our local synagogue with the Jews. Then he branched out and reached the Gentiles. He was something else—people couldn't remain neutral about him. He generated both followers and enemies at the same time.

Then, after 18 months of this preaching, some of the leading Jews in Corinth hauled him before the judge and accused him of spreading a false gospel. The charges were dismissed, but Paul thought it best to get out of town. So we closed up shop, and the three of us bought tickets for Ephesus.

What a sight as we sailed into the harbor. We immediately spotted the huge temple erected to worship Artemis—you may recall her as "Diana." Her temple was so huge it was considered to be one of the seven wonders of our ancient world.

It didn't take Paul long before we had enough converts with which to start another church. He left us behind to co-pastor this new church while he sailed on to other places that needed to hear the gospel for the first time. He was one focused man. He was aflame and wanted to shine the light of the Word everywhere.

Before long, another Jewish evangelist came into our town. He was eloquent, he was gifted, and he was personable, but there was a slight problem with his doctrine. He was preaching a simple message much like John the Baptist. Apollos didn't have all the understanding of the whole gospel. He was well educated and came from Alexandria, the learning capital of the world, but there was a gap in his knowledge.

We talked it out and together Aquila and I went to him, not to condemn him but to give him further instruction in the faith. He was a quick learner and wanted to hear everything Paul had taught us. I must say we did the job so well that our church elders sent Apollos to Corinth to hold more meetings to help that church move to the next level.

It was a fulfilling and satisfying life we had together as a team under the direction of Paul. It was soon evident that God had gifted my husband and me with a teaching ministry. We traveled as a team wherever there was a need. To have been privileged to help lead the infant church was a remarkable opportunity we were so thankful to have had.

We learned how to trust God in any and all kinds of circumstances, even when our lives were threatened with violence and death. I discovered that our faith grew out of the soil of controversy and hostility. We didn't give up nor shrivel up—the more persecution, the move effective the gospel became. It was a joy to risk life and limb for the sake of the gospel of Jesus Christ we loved so much.

I believe my role as a disciple and teacher in the church set a new standard for women everywhere. Paul reminded me often, "Priscilla, there are not Jews or Greeks, slaves or free people, and most importantly there is no distinction between men or women; we are all one because of Jesus Christ!" Now, women, don't forget that! Paul knocked down the barriers of race, status in life, and even gender. He insisted that there was to be no first-class or low-class people. We are all one because of what Jesus Christ bought for all of us on the cross. It was a message he kept repeating wherever he went. The religious leaders hated this message and did all they could to stop Paul and the rest of us Christians.

But it was like throwing lamp oil on a fire—the gospel just spread. The greater the opposition, the greater and farther the message went.

Many of our churches' earliest leaders ended their lives in

martyrdom. I'm not sure why Aquila and I were spared a violent death. But to our dying day, we were faithful at teaching the word of truth until the Lord took us home. What a life we lived, and what a wonderful privilege to have lived it for the Lord!

WISDOM FOR 21ST CENTURY LIVING
FROM PRISCILLA...

Paul wrote the epitaph for my life with these words: "Greet Priscilla and Aquila, my fellow workers in Christ Jesus. They risked their lives for me. Not only I but all the churches of the Gentiles are grateful to them" (Romans 16:3-4). We could never have receive a better compliment.

Can I be so bold as to encourage you? Build your home with your spouse as a partnership. Everything we did in life and ministry, we did it together as a team. We had different roles, but were equals in business, equals in our chosen lifestyle, equals in ministry, and equals in our love for the Lord. I wish for you this kind of a home!

Chapter Nineteen

LYDIA

Desperate for more of God

Lydia was an Asiatic from the region of Thyatira and the city of Lydia where people were called "Lydians." The name "Lydia" was quite popular for women of her day. Her real name may not have actually been Lydia, but Luke identified her as Lydia or "the Lydian."

Nothing more of her background is given, and we surmise from the biblical record she was either a widow or single woman. She was also a wealthy business woman running a factory making dyed cloth; her specialty seemed to be purples. Her town was a melting pot of peoples of many nations and cultures. Thyatira was one of the Macedonia colonies and the center of the Apollo sun-god worship. There also was a strong Jewish element there who kept their faith in Jehovah.

Scripture: *Acts 16:6-40; Philippians 1:1-10*

HER SIDE OF THE STORY...

We were having our weekly women's meeting down by the river banks. Since we didn't even have ten eligible and reliable men to form a synagogue in Philippi, some of us women got together weekly. Our gathering took place in a local tea shop or somebody's home. My favorite place was on the banks of our river. We were just a handful of faithful women, some were Jewish and some were Gentiles like me, who gathered each Sabbath to pray. I really wanted to know all about the one God.

The day was wonderful—a slight breeze rustled the leaves in the tree under which we sat. The river was gently babbling; the birds were singing; all was well with the world. This particular Sabbath we had some visitors; the leader was from Tarsus and he and his small band of followers found us. They were looking for a place to get some peace and quiet, and we were praying, so they joined us. This guy began with words familiar to all of us, the *shema*, "Hear, O Israel: The Lord our God, the Lord is one…" There was something that stirred inside of me as this man named Paul prayed. I was a spiritually hungry Gentile who had come to Philippi from Asia-Minor. I had moved my business to this location because it was near to some of the raw materials I needed in my business.

I also wanted to know more about this God of Israel who could part the waters of the Red Sea and do other miraculous acts. In the course of doing business, I had met some Jewish women who invited me to be a part of their small group. Eagerly I went, and they taught me about the God of Abraham, Isaac, and Jacob, but I always wanted to know more.

Paul didn't stop with shema; he began to speak of their God who had sent his one and only Son, Jesus Christ of Nazareth, who had been crucified by the Romans. This same Jesus, after three days being dead and in a tomb, miraculously came back to life. This was the Messiah who had come to live among people, die for them, and rise again so they would know him as the one and only true God.

We were mesmerized by Paul's teaching. As he continued, I couldn't help myself, and tears began rolling down my cheeks. Something wonderful was working on my insides; I felt like getting up and dancing for joy. I believed in this Messiah! I was ready to live for him.

I was not the only one. I looked at my servants who had come with me, and they were crying. The Jewish ladies with us were crying too. It's as though God opened the doors of our hearts and walked right in. It was glorious! I made my decision to follow this Christ.

Paul told us the next step was to be baptized in water because of our repentance and conversion. Since we were sitting on the banks of the river, we all decided to get baptized right then. Even though it was the dirty Gangites River, all my household were baptized with me along with the Jewish ladies. What a time we had worshipping and praising the new-found Lord.

I insisted that Paul, Silas, Timothy, and Luke come to my home and stay with me. They accepted my hospitality, and my cook served up the most delicious meals.

Paul and his men continued preaching and teaching in our town until we had established a church with many believers. It was my joy and privilege to have a small part in this new church; in fact, it started in my home until we outgrew it.

I must tell you what happened next, although you may have already heard about it. One day as we all were on our way to the place of prayer, a girl began following us and shouting, "These people are servants of the Most High God who are telling you the way to be saved!" Everywhere we went, she followed and shouted at the top of her lungs. It went on for many days, and I noticed it bothered Paul who really didn't want a confrontation.

Finally, Paul had enough. He turned around and commanded the evil spirit in the girl: "In the name of Jesus Christ, I command you to come out of her!" Instantly, she was delivered and in her right mind! She became another convert and staunch follower of Christ.

I noticed this didn't sit well with her owners. You see, they had been using her to tell fortunes, read palms, and do horoscopes. She was their meal ticket. When the girl was worshipping Jesus who had set her free, her owners saw it was hopeless. She would be no further good for them!

They grabbed Paul and Silas and dragged them before the city council who believed their story. The mayor ordered them to be stripped and flogged and thrown into solitary confinement with their feet in stocks.

About midnight, when Paul and Silas were singing and praising God and preaching to all the other prisoners, the power of God fell and there was a violent earthquake. The foundations were shaken, the doors flew open, and all the chains and stocks fell off, releasing their prisoners.

The jailer, in his quarters right next to the prison, was also rudely awakened. He came running and when he saw the doors wide open, he was sure they had all escaped. As a result, he knew the authorities would take his life. Quickly, he yanked out his sword from the scabbard and was about to fall on it when Paul saw him and shouted, "Don't kill yourself! All the prisoners are still here!"

The jailer called for the torches to be brought and ran back to where Paul and Silas were and fell on his face in front of them. He knew it was only because of them that the prisoners were still there.

He brought Paul and Silas outside and demanded, "What do I have to do to be saved?"

Their answer was pointed, simplicity itself, "Believe in the Lord Jesus, and you will be saved—you and your household!"

Within the hour, the jailer and his whole family, servants also, were saved. How do we know? The jailer immediately washed and dressed their wounds from the flogging, then they all went to the river and were baptized, in the middle of the night. Then they had a very early breakfast! The jailer and his family were rejoicing.

About dawn, the city council members sent their police officers to the jailer with orders: "Release those two men!" It makes me wonder if all of the council members and the mayor had a bit of an earthquake-shaking time, too!

The jailer passed this order along to Paul and Silas's guards who told them, "You are free to go."

But Paul said to the officers: "Your city council members had us beaten publicly without a trial. Tell them that we are Roman citizens. They threw us in prison, and now they want to get rid of us. They want us to sneak out of town. No! Let them come in person and escort us out of this jail in broad daylight, in full view of the townspeople!" Just because Paul was a Christian did not mean he was a wimp!

The officers got to the council chambers and relayed Paul's message—talk about people quaking in their boots! Meekly every council member along with the mayor came with their heads down. They did everything they could to appease Paul and Silas. I secretly think Paul really enjoyed this moment. I thought I detected a slight twitching of his lips, almost a smile. Finally, Paul was willing to leave. By this time, word had spread about what had happened, and the people flocked to catch the fun and take a look at the jail that had been ruined by the quake.

The mayor politely asked Paul, "Now, will you please quietly leave this city? I don't want any more trouble...please."

Paul nodded his head and said, "Let's go!"

You should have seen this little parade. The mayor led the way, waving to the crowd, smiling, and attempting to make the best of a bad situation. Paul and Silas came out next, singing a duet, "When the saints come marching out...oh when the saints come marching out..." What a moment!

And Paul led the way for all the spectators to my house for a celebration brunch! You could tell that Paul was on top of his game. He met all the brothers with a hug and handshake and a kiss. It was a moving moment as he encouraged all of us not to give up the fight!

When I look back on those early days of our church, Philippi would seem a most unlikely place to plant a new church. It was a wicked, wide-open kind of town similar to a frontier gold mining town because gold had been discovered in the mountains to the north of the city. It had been named for Philip II, who was father to Alexander the Great, and was a prosperous colony for the Romans. It was right on a main highway connecting all of the eastern provinces with Rome. It was changed forever by Paul's visit.

You know his visit came about because of a dream or vision he had. A man appeared in the night and begged, "Come to Macedonia and help us!" That's how he found himself on a river bank preaching to a bunch of women who were having their weekly prayer meeting. I should also tell you that these women became the foundation and backbone of the church here.

WISDOM FOR 21ST CENTURY LIVING
FROM A WOMAN BUSINESS TYCOON...

Ladies, when my husband died and left me with the business, I really didn't know how to carry on. But you know what, I discovered strengths and gifts I never knew I had. If tragedy hits your home, you can make it; with God's help, you can do the impossible!

Please be open to the truth about the Gospel of Jesus Christ. Those empty longings inside, that hunger when no one else is around is an opening for a God who is still touching lives with his forgiveness. There's a void inside that nothing else can fill other than a relationship with your Creator.

And remember, you have influence beyond yourself. My entire household followed my lead in accepting Christ and being baptized.

Use your gifts of hospitality to make life a bit better for one or more of God's choice servants. The reward in giving was mine. I know my thoughtfulness blessed Paul and his traveling companions, but I was blessed more in return by their presence.

Chapter Twenty

THE MOTHER-IN-LAW

Desperate for a healing

 This nameless mother-in-law is only known because of her famous son-in-law. She is Peter's wife's mother, and we don't even know the name of Peter's wife. After Peter was married, his mother-in-law lived with them. Paul wrote in a letter (I Corinthians 9:5) that his wife accompanied him on some of his missionary journeys and took care of his many needs.

The Bible doesn't tell us if Andrew, Peter's brother, was married. But it tells us that he lived in the same house with Peter and Peter's wife and the mother-in-law. They had a house in Bethsaida or Capernaum, likely because of their father's legacy.

Mothers-in-law have taken a bad rap, but in an ancient Middle-Eastern setting, it usually was a happy domestic relationship.

Scripture: *Matthew 8:14-18; Mark 1:29-34; Luke 4:38-41*

HER SIDE OF THE STORY...

I will tell you this right up front, I loved my son-in-law and he loved me, and we got along just fine. Ours happened to be a happy, multi-generational home, and all of us enjoyed and loved each other most of the time. With that said, let's get on with my story.

Life was good for Jake and me. We were a typical Jewish family and raised six kids—three boys and three girls. And if I say so myself, they all turned out to be good citizens and married well. Honestly, there were times when I had my doubts, but time has proven me out, they turned out to be good people.

Naomi was our oldest; she was real pretty and there were lots of suitors who came calling. She had this signal worked out between her and her father. If she didn't approve, she just gently shook her head "no" and her dad always got her off the hook. Remember that marriages in our day were "arranged" and involved a lot of eastern-type bargaining to set a dowry and other details. It worked well for us. Don't think for a minute that we women didn't have a say in whom we wanted to marry. When our girls had a good relationship with their fathers and mothers, it all worked out just right. After all, we parents wanted the very best for our children.

Our Naomi was very fussy. Lots of prospective suitors came and all of them got the "no" nod from her until one day, Zebedee, the father of a big, burly fisherman, came to us. Our Naomi had been spending some time on the shores of the lake, telling us she was fishing, but really it was a ruse to check out a man named Simon. She liked what she saw and apparently he liked what he saw too.

There was all kinds of excitement in our house when Zebedee came calling. Sparks of excitement exploded out Naomi's eyes at the possibility. She nodded "Yes, yes, yes...Daddy, please!"

Well, bold and brash Simon became my first son-in-law! I, too, learned to love him, warts and all. But he sure was fun to be with. You never knew what he might do next. He was a great practical joker and loved to kid me. We had a great relationship. He was tough and yet tender at the same time. For a man, he was sensitive and could get his feelings hurt, which he'd never admit. It wasn't macho for men to show tender feelings. He was an excellent provider—his family business was fishing with his dad and Andrew his brother, plus they had a bunch of hired people as well. So he lived well; we all lived well.

Time went on, and the rest of our kids married and started families. What a delight to see them mature! Being a grandmother was so much fun. But Simon was still my favorite son-in-law; he was a huge teddy-bear of a guy.

For me, the passing away of my husband changed my lifestyle because, as a widow, my status was different. Simon and my Naomi invited me to move into their large, comfortable home. Even though I missed my husband, it proved to be a happy time in my life. I pitched right in and carried my load, especially with the cooking and entertaining. It seemed as though we always had a bunch of visitors; suspiciously many of them seemed to pick meal times for their visits. I'd like to think it was my cooking that became the main attraction.

The latest buzz all centered about this young man, Jesus, who some said was the Messiah. This news caused quite a stir and caused us all to be curious. John the Baptist had been preaching for quite a while and promised the Messiah would be coming soon. We understood that Jesus and John were cousins and had grown up together. John became the most famous evangelist in our land, but soon Jesus was the center of attraction. We avidly listened as we learned of his baptism, his time in the wilderness, how they rejected him, and his preaching in his home town of Nazareth. It was the news of the land. His preaching was powerful but so were the stories of healings and people's deliverance from evil spirits.

One day Simon heard him preaching in the synagogue and invited Jesus to come over for dinner. Wait a minute…I'm a bit ahead of myself. Just a day or two before this invitation was given, I had come down with a high fever, and the doctors were helpless. It was serious. I was out of my head with the fever. Doctors shook their heads and said, "It's hopeless, just make her comfortable. There's nothing we can do. In fact, if we are honest with you, we don't think she'll make it."

Back to the story—Simon, bless his generous heart, was always being the hospitable host. We never knew who he might bring home with him—stray dogs or stray people. Jesus was his guest this day.

As usual we had a house full and now Jesus on top of this. This was to be the first time we had an opportunity to check him out personally. So when Jesus arrived, even before they could wash his feet like good hosts, some of them asked Jesus to help me, the sick one.

He said, "Sure, where is she?"

They brought him into my bedroom, and I'll never forget what happened next. He bent over to look me in the eye, then took my hand, and simply said, "Fever! Be gone! Leave this moment!" Then, he lifted me up to my feet. I was completely healed, instantly well! In fact I felt so invigorated that I went right to the kitchen and began preparing and serving them supper! Of course, I served Jesus first—what a man! Yes, we all believed that he was the promised Messiah. What a moment in our history. Imagine, him in our house!

It was unbelievable, but you know how we Jews are—can't keep a secret and can't keep good news to ourselves! The details of my healing flew through our village, and by sunset, there were hundreds of people bringing all kinds of sick people to our house. Some people were blind, others crippled, some deaf, some badly injured, some riding in wheelchairs, others on cots, and many demon-possessed. It was incredible how Jesus went through this crowd, laying his hands on them and praying a short, simple prayer! Every one he touched was healed! The demons came out shouting, "You are the Son of God!" And Jesus refused them to say any more. Never in my life had there been such a happy, glorious day. Not only was I healed instantly, but all the sick in our town were healed too. We danced and shouted and wept and celebrated Jesus and all he had done. What a night it was!

Finally, Jesus had a few short hours to catch some sleep. Then he went down to the shore of the Galilee for some solitude. Wouldn't you know it, somebody found him and spread the word and the crowds came. This time they begged him to stay in our town.

Gently, he told them, "I must preach this gospel of good news to other towns because this was the reason my heavenly Father has sent me."

He came back to our house for a light brunch and then he was on his way. How I loved that man! There was something so magnetic about him, something I had never sensed in another person. He sure changed my life.

Well the story isn't ended yet. Jesus preached in synagogues all over Judea and then returned to our part of the lake. He just appeared and the word spread and the people shouted to one another, "He's back! He's preaching down on the lakeshore!" They didn't even have to say who "he" was; people just knew. This was "the man!"

So many people crowded around that he jumped into Simon's boat and had him paddle out a little ways so everyone could hear him continue preaching. His voice carried over the water, just like having loud speakers.

You'll never believe what happened next. When he had finished preaching, he told my Simon, "Let's go out a little deeper and let down your nets for a catch."

Simon, bless his heart, told the Master in so many words he didn't know what he was doing. "Master, we fished all night and didn't catch anything. Now you, who are not a fisherman, are telling me to let down the nets for a catch? But because you, the miracle-working one, are asking, I will do it just to prove to you there are no fish in this spot!"

Down went the nets and almost immediately they were filled to overflowing with wet, flopping fish! They attempted to get the nets in their boat, but they were breaking because there were too many fish filling them! They shouted to another boat, "Get over here, quick! We've got more fish than we can handle! Hurry!" They had such a catch that both boats began to sink!

Finally, the Lord had really gotten through to my thick-headed Simon! My healing had not been enough to really convince him. He fell on his knees at the feet of Jesus and blurted, "Get away from me, Lord; I have been an unbelieving sinful man!" He got a bit mixed up, he really meant, "Lord forgive me of my sins and unbelief." He really didn't want Jesus to run from him; he wanted more of Jesus.

The men jumped overboard and finally beached their boats, full of fish and all their equipment. They were all on shore marveling over the miracle catch—one of the biggest fish stories ever to happen on our lake. You should have heard how this story spread and grew as fish stories are prone to do.

Jesus looked Simon in the eye, "Don't be afraid; don't worry; follow me, and from now on I will teach you how to catch people!" That day, that moment, Peter and his brother left everything and followed Jesus. He stopped by the house and told Naomi what he was doing. He gave her a big hug and kiss and was off on the greatest adventure any man in world history was to have.

Jesus eventually had 12 disciples, whom he mentored and

who went everywhere with him. Whenever they needed a nourishing home-cooked meal, they stopped by our house. What a happy bunch of guys. Those were great days. Jesus was the most joyful person I had ever met, and his joy filled the twelve.

I should also tell you Jesus changed Simon's name into "Peter, the Rock." Oh, he wasn't really the rock yet, but eventually he did become Peter the Rock, the leader of the Church. It's more of a story than I have time to tell you. But you should know how it all ended.

There was the crucifixion and the resurrection. Peter denied his Lord and was he filled with remorse and guilt! He came home to a place of refuge where his beloved Naomi helped him to put it all in perspective. Then there was the special breakfast when Jesus appeared to Peter and the others. Peter in despair had finally said, "I'm going back to fishing," but Jesus had other plans for Peter and the guys.

The day of Pentecost came, and there were more than 120 of us who had been praying for a number of days for the "Comforter" that Jesus had promised when he left us. Tongues of fire and a rushing wind filled the place and all of us. This prayer meeting spilled out into the streets and a huge crowd gathered. Nothing like this outpouring had ever happened before. And my Peter, my forgiven Peter, stood and preached like Jesus had taught him. Would you believe it—more than 3000 people believed and were baptized that day! Peter had really become that "fisher of men" Jesus had prophesied he would become. He became the first pastor of the first church of Jerusalem. Soon it numbered in the thousands, which was a phenomenon in our day. This was followed by many missionary journeys so that eventually the gospel was spread across the world.

Eventually, Peter was arrested for preaching the gospel, and

Naomi was also captured. I was still at home taking care of the house and the kids and all the others who needed a momma or grandma.

I just need to tell how it all ended. Peter escaped from the prison in Rome with the help of some of the Christians who were part of Caesar's palace. We never did find out how this happened. Anyway Peter is on the open road and making good time away from Rome when he was stopped by a vision or special appearance of our Lord. Peter, ever bold and brash asked, "Lord, where are you going and why are you here?" Just like Peter.

The Lord gently replied, "Peter, I am on my way to Rome to be crucified a second time." Peter was humiliated. He caught the message. He turned around and made his way back to the prison from which he had escaped. He had a death sentence hanging over his head. This didn't matter.

First, they brutally brought out Naomi to where Peter was held in chains and asked Peter to recant his preaching. If he did this, she would go free. Through tears, he refused. They gave him and her a few fleeting moments. Peter tenderly said, "My love. Remember our Lord. Remember me." They yanked her away and in full sight of him and the public, beheaded her.

Next was Peter's turn. He begged them, "Please crucify me upside down, with my head down because I am not worthy to die like my Lord died." They honored his request.

I can only imagine what kind of a reunion these two shared that day in heaven!

WISDOM FOR 21ST CENTURY LIVING FROM A MOTHER-IN-LAW...

To be a loved and loving mother-in-law will take some practice and restraint. Learn to keep your mouth shut when it comes to interjecting yourself in the affairs of a new home. You are the mother of the bride or groom and as such you've had your say, so turn the newlyweds loose and let them fly on their own. If you live under the same roof, remember you are a guest in a home other than yours. Pray for your newlyweds.

In my case, the only answer to my sickness was a touch from the Master. I remind you again, He cares for you and all aspects of your life and the life of your child. Build your home on the life-giving principles of Jesus and the Word of God. And believe your children will do the same when it comes time for them to set up housekeeping.

Chapter Twenty-One

JOANNA

Desperate to use her wealth

Joanna was in the close circle of women disciples who followed Jesus. Her name means, "the Lord gives graciously" or "The Lord is grace." Like so many women mentioned in the Bible, we know almost nothing about her family and background but can only speculate.

We do know that she was the wife of Chuza, who was the man who managed the considerable property holdings of King Herod Antipas. He and his wife were considered nobility, a part of the privileged ruling class, and quite wealthy. There is some speculation that Chuza was in fact the nobleman John wrote about (John 4:46-54) with the sick son who was healed. As a result of the miraculous healing, this nobleman and his family and household servants became believers along with his wife Joanna. It seems logical.

Scripture: *Luke 8:1-3; 23:55; 24:10* (Some more reading on Herod and the background on his court and how it functioned can be found in *Matthew 14:1-12; Luke 23:7-12)*

HER SIDE OF THE STORY...

I was fortunately born into wealth and married into more

wealth. I lived in the high-society of my day—a heady as well as a worldly, pampered lifestyle. They were the upper-crust of our day.

Living at the center of power, you soon learn how to sail through the troubled waters of constant intrigue about the king's throne. Really, it was a brutal way to live, and only the strong and well-connected survived. I learn the art of survival quite young and wielded my powers frequently. The word was out, "Don't mess with this Joanna woman!" I reveled in my reputation. "Beauty with brains" was my little mantra. Next to the king, my Chuza and I were the most powerful people in the kingdom. The king was the king but Chuza was COO, "chief operating officer," and nothing got to Herod without going through my man. Therefore I had direct access to the reins of power, and I loved it! In your democratic world, you would not be able to fathom the opulent lifestyle of the wealthy Romans. It was a heady lifestyle, and I did everything to protect it and use it. Life in this stratosphere of human existence was dog-eat-dog. You had to be on top of your game at all times.

I thought I was immune to the sadistic brutality of Herod's reign, but it made me really sick. I couldn't take the sight of John the Baptist's head on a silver platter! The holiest man in Israel was murdered because he told the truth! That was the moment I began to question my long held beliefs.

Just a few short weeks passed, and our oldest son got sick while at our summer home in Capernaum. Chuza and I helplessly watched him waste away. We had the best doctors check him out, but they all shook their heads in frustration and told us to prepare for his imminent death. As parents we were frantic. We spent our days and nights at his bedside while he grew progressively sicker.

We had discussed the possibility of getting him to the

healer, Jesus, whom everybody was talking about. We had never seen him, but we were assured by many of his miraculous powers. Finally, having exhausted all avenues for help, we decided to go to this Jesus, this friend of sinners and lower caste types, even if it felt humiliating. Our son was too sick to be taken anywhere, so Chuza went to find him, and I stayed behind desperately trying to take care of our son.

Chuza caught up to Jesus in Cana in Galilee, incidentally, the place where he had turned water into wine. Chuza approached Jesus in as humble a way as he knew how. "Master, please, would you come to our summer palace and heal our son? He's real close to death."

Jesus replied, "Unless people like you, privileged people, see miraculous signs, you'll never believe." That stopped Chuza for a moment, but not for long because in his position you had to think on your feet.

Chuza just simply plowed on ahead and repeated, "Master, please go with me before he dies."

Jesus replied, "You can go. You don't need me in person. Your son will live!" Somehow Chuza believed him, maybe because he had to read people who attempted to deceive or lie to him. He was a great lie detector, but he believed this Jesus. He took him at his word and got in his chariot and returned home.

Meanwhile, I was sitting at the bedside of our dying son who was now in a deep coma, barely breathing. Suddenly, he sat bolt upright in bed and said, "Mom, Mom, I'm hungry! Get me something to eat!" Just like that! He jumped out of bed and ran to the kitchen with me hurrying to catch up.

This was great news! A couple of our servants were so excited they saddled up a couple of horses and galloped off to meet my husband with the good news.

Chuza asked, "Exactly, when did this happen?"

"The fever was instantly gone yesterday at the seventh hour!"

Chuza, astonished, said, "That's the exact time Jesus said to me, 'Your son will live.'" Chuza had a little victory celebration with the servants right in the middle of the road.

They hurried home, and Chuza gave a strong, healthy boy a hug only a loving father could bestow to a son who had come back to life. It was a glorious time, and as a result, all of us, family and household servants and all our hired help became believers! I told everyone about the miracle of healing, even King Herod and the scheming Herodias. I told as many as would listen.

Then it struck me like lightning! What could I do to help the Master in such a way as to free him from some of the normal everyday worries such as, what to eat, what to wear, where to go, where to stay? I wanted to free him from the mundane so he could concentrate on his ministry to the masses. I volunteered and became a lady disciple. I freely and generously gave out of my wealth to make life a bit easier for him and the twelve. And Chuza agreed with me that this was the right thing to do. It became our ministry of love.

After our son was healed, I knew I also needed healing. My condition was not that critical. I wasn't yet at death's door, but I was facing a rapidly growing sickness in my body. So it was decided it would be my turn to go to Jesus like Chuza had gone. Well, it happened again! As Jesus was praying for all kinds of people with all kinds of needs, he touched me and pronounced me as being healed! It happened instantly, just like my son. I was whole again with all my life energies restored. What a time!

Back to my discipleship and ministry of hospitality. So many miraculous things happened, I can't begin to tell you. One event stands out. It was when a crowd, I'd estimate the entire crowd, counting women and kids as well as the men, were more than twenty thousand. It was meal time and people had been so excited to see Jesus, they forgot to pack lunches.

The ladies who were in charge, that's me and the others, agreed there was no way could we feed this large bunch. The only lunch anywhere was a small boy who had five small buns and two small fish—only enough for this boy. How Andrew had found him, I don't know. But he brought him to Jesus and explained our plight. There was no food and the people were about to faint from hunger.

Jesus, ever in command of each situation, said, "Have them sit down in rows and groups." Then he took the little boy's lunch and held the buns and fish in his hands and gave thanks for the food we were about to eat. He gave buns and fish to his disciples and had them distribute them to everybody. Seconds were available...and some people exclaimed, "That's the best fish I've ever had, please give me another!" Talk about a party. The more they ate, the more food there was until everybody had been served, most of them more than once! I must admit I had the best gourmet cook in the kingdom, but not even he could turn out fish like Jesus did. I tried to have him duplicate the taste later, but he never could get it right. It must have been some of that heavenly spice with a touch of honey or something else out of this world!

Then, Jesus told us to gather up the fragments to clean the area. Altogether they gathered 12 baskets full, which he sent home with the needy and the little boy who took a whole basket back home to his momma and daddy. I wonder what they thought as he told them what had happened!

Needless to say, every day held surprises and miracles. I was part of his support group for more than two years. It all came to a screeching stop when he was arrested, tried, beaten and crucified. It was a sad day. I watched it all to the end, even when they put him in a tomb and sealed it up.

The men all ran away, but we women planned to come back on the first day of the next week to do a proper embalming. We purchased spices and really costly perfumes. I told my Chuza and our son every detail of those sad days.

We rested on the Sabbath and early on Sunday, we made our way back to the tomb. It was awesome! You know our story. Some of us ran back to Jerusalem to tell the disciples what we had seen and experienced, but they dismissed us as the ravings of some hysterical women. I had no doubts, and all of the other women had no doubts! I know all about power, but the resurrection was a much greater power! Imagine the power . it would take to make someone come back alive after being dead for three days!

Yes, I was highly privileged to have been one of the first witnesses of the resurrection of Jesus Christ, the King of all kings and the Lord of all lords! My Savior, my Redeemer, my friend, my healer, and He will do the same for you!

WISDOM FOR 21ST CENTURY LIVING FROM A LADY OF NOBILITY...

I learned the positive truth: "Weeping may endure for the night, but joy comes in the morning!" On Resurrection day, I came from a night of weeping and grieving only to have all of that turned into joy! The truth is, even if your weeping lasts for many nights, don't give up. Eventually your joy will arrive.

The Savior of Life has promised it could happen tomorrow, or at the end of a day, or even at the end of life, but there will be a joy-filled morning for all of us who have placed our trust in Him who is the resurrection and the life!

When I began following Jesus, I quickly understood his teaching, "It's more blessed to give than it is to receive." The more I gave, the more I wanted to give.

Chapter Twenty-Two

DORCAS

Desperate to live again

Dorcas is the first Greek name of a woman in the New Testament. The Hebrew translation of her name is "Tabitha," a name given to girls today. It means "the female roebuck" or simply "a gazelle," a symbol of beauty and graceful movements.

Dorcas lived in the town of Joppa located about 35 miles northwest of Jerusalem right on the coast of the Mediterranean Sea. As so many other biblical women, we know nothing about her background. She apparently was a single woman, most likely a widow. She was known in her town for her many acts of kindness such as providing clothes to others in need. Today there is a group of philanthropists named the "Dorcas Society."

Scripture: *Acts 9:32-42*

HER SIDE OF THE STORY...

What do you think is the ultimate life experience any human being can have? My vote is for dying and coming back to life! That's my story, but there is much more to it.

Let me start at the beginning: my life was pretty typical for a Jewish woman. I grew up, married, and created a pleasant home with my husband. It was a good life with regular rhythms and cycles. There was nothing out of the ordinary that would interest you. When our kids grew up and left home, we traveled and enjoyed our freedom until my husband died of a heart attack. Life took an about-face. Fortunately my husband had prepared well for this time in my life, and so, for a widow, I lived very well. I began spending my time as a volunteer helping the sick. In addition I began sewing clothes for the poor widows in our group.

The most exciting new thing in Joppa was when these new Christian missionaries came to our town and created a church. I became one of the charter members and, eventually, head of the Ladies Sewing Circle group. We quilted and sewed clothes for many needy ladies, especially widows. In fact, our church had the best dressed senior women you would ever see any-place. Word spread far and wide about our helping ministry.

We also helped out the many traveling evangelists and mis-sionaries who stopped by our church. It was a labor of love that became a model for other churches to follow.

Soon I began to find myself short of breath and running out of steam long before my day was done. I was one of those "type A" people you hear about: always on the move, always doing something, never stopping, just busy, busy, busy. This lack of strength began to cramp my style. Soon it worsened and I went to our local clinic, but there was no real help there. They didn't know why I felt that way. Their diagnosis was to get more rest, stay off my feet, and they wished me "good luck." My condition worsened. One doctor speculated it had something to do with a bad heart, but I still received no help.

The next step was to get complete bed rest and depend on the help of my friends. How I appreciated all of them.

Then, I died, although I don't remember it. My friends tell me that I went into a coma and passed away in my sleep. My memory is really vague about what happened. I had an experience that was full of light and wonderful, but the specifics I can't recall. All I know is that I will not fear death again.

Life, outside my house, was going on as always—the winds continued to blow in off the ocean, and the waves rolled on the beach. Friends, family, neighbors, and my group of widows all came to mourn. Mourning in the Middle East was a despairing racket of wailing and weeping. If there were not enough mourners and the noise level wasn't high enough, the family hired professional mourners to add to the chaos. We didn't handle death very well, but it was a cleaning, a catharsis. We recovered quickly and, after the period of mourning, life went on.

But for a Christian, death was something different. We knew God could do the impossible, and we had heard of the resurrection of our Lord as well as stories of people being raised back to life: Jarius's daughter, the boy in a funeral procession, Lazarus, and more. Since Jesus had left us, there had been more reports of resurrections. We all believed it could and would happen again.

So when the disciples got word of my death, they quickly sent two of them to get Peter who was preaching in Lydda. He was having quite a revival meeting—Aeneas, a paralytic bedridden for eight years, had been completely healed. As a result, every person in Lydda and Sharon became believers!

By this time I was dead. My body was washed and prepared for burial in an upstairs room in my house and waiting for Peter's arrival. Peter hurried, but I was already dead!

Peter and two others heard the noise of the mourners a long time before they neared the house. Quickly he climbed up the stairs only to be met by a roomful of weeping widows. All of these ladies showed him the clothes I had made for them.

Peter saw these women weren't ready to pray the prayer of faith with him, so he hustled all of them out of the room. "Take your weeping out of this room!" he said.

Peter then knelt down beside my bed and began to pray. I don't know how long, but it was effective! I had heard that he hadn't even prayed for Aeneas but only said, "Aeneas, Jesus Christ heals you! Now get up and roll up your sleeping bag! Get on with life!"

Peter had prayed with his back to me. Why? I really believe he was picturing me in his mind of faith as being alive, not seeing me as being dead. Then he turned and said, "Tabitha, get up!"

That's the first thing I had heard. My eyes popped open! *It's Peter; what's he doing here? This is not heaven!* He gave me his hand and helped me to get out of the bed and stand!

Together we started down the stairs and Peter called, loudly, so he could be heard over their wailing, "Come and take a look." Then he held my hand, and with a slight bow, said, "It's my honor and privilege to present to you the new, the wonderful, the glorious, the seamstress, the new Tabitha!"

They clapped, they shouted, they cried, but there was no more sorrowful wailing. It was purely a moment of joy! We hugged and celebrated. It's not every day you have somebody come back from the other side. And the questions never stopped.

Word spread like wildfire. The people came running because they all wanted to see me alive again. And revival came to our town because of my miracle. Each night in the meetings I was asked to share about my experience. What excitement, what a demonstration of the power of God still at work, even though Jesus had been taken from us.

The next day, just at dawn, I climbed to the patio on my rooftop. What a wonderful time of day. I looked up and down the beach which adjoined my property in the back, and it was littered with driftwood. I deeply inhaled the salty sea air. Some how it was different. It was almost as though before I had never really seen the beauty around me.

But there was almost a strange longing inside I could not explain. I had been to an even better place, a place of brilliant clear light, a place of such a wonderful deep peace, a place totally controlled by the presence of God. I was happy to return to the earth and my friends and my church and my ministry, but there is a palpable hunger to return some day to my eternal home.

I sighed, turned, and climbed back downstairs. I had things waiting for me to do: unfinished clothing projects to complete, bread to bake for the hungry, Bible study to prepare for our next meeting, and a visit to make to a shut-in widow. I was busy, but in the middle of the bustle of a busy life, there was that unsatisfied desire for the other world. In fact, I can tell you this longing seemed to increase as the days went by. It was something nobody could really understand. It was a wonderful privilege that few people ever experience. After all, how many people do you know who have died and come back to tell about it? Not many, I bet.

Life went on, but the longing never subsided. It changed my entire outlook on life. I learned to really appreciate the present moment. I learned to love others with a different kind of love.

I continued with my life dedicated to performing practical acts of love and kindness for others.

And yes, like Lazarus and all the others who had been raised from the dead, I too eventually died again! But it was a passing I welcomed for it was the doorway to heaven and home. I welcomed it the second time.

WISDOM FOR 21ST CENTURY LIVING
FROM A RESURRECTED WOMAN...

Really, there is one lesson that stands out from all the rest in my life: Death awaits for all of us sooner or later. You must make preparations for this event. Where will you spend it eternity—heaven or hell? You decide here on this earth.

"God so loved the world that he gave his one and only Son, that whoever believes in him shall not perish but have eternal life. For God did not send his Son into the world to condemn the world, but to save the world through him" (John 3:16-17).

Exactly how do we believe and how are we saved? Again, the plan is perfectly clear, If you confess with your mouth, "Jesus is Lord," and believe in your heart that God raised him from the dead, you will be saved. For it is with your heart that you believe, and it is with your mouth that you confess and are saved. As the Scripture says, "Anyone who trusts in him will never be put to shame" (Romans 10:9-11).

If you have never made this decision or prayed a prayer of decision, how about praying with me the following: "Dear Lord, I believe that Jesus Christ is real and that God raised him from the dead. I now confess with my mouth that Jesus is Lord and he died for my sins! I accept the fact that I am now made right. I declare I am saved. I put my trust in You! Thank you for hearing my prayer and making me a part of the family of God. Amen!"

If this is the first time you have prayed this prayer, or maybe it is a renewing of your relationship with Jesus, let me ask you to do the following:

Tell someone about your decision to believe in Jesus Christ. Begin reading your Bible...God's Word to you. Begin to attend a Bible-believing and preaching church. Begin a regular Bible reading and prayer time each day.

EPILOGUE

Have you noticed any kind of common link or emerging patterns in the lives of most of these women? What of your life? Are you a desperate woman? Are you looking for answers? Is your life a shambles? Maybe there's only one area that you have having problems with or maybe you consider it all a disaster.

The majority of these vignettes paint a picture of these women as they related to Jesus Christ. They had all kinds of human problems: sickness, death, frustrating relationships, dead children, being outcasts, and more. Each found an answer when they came to Jesus or one of his representatives.

Jesus highly valued women and elevated them to first-class status. Historically, wherever Christianity has advanced, women are set free and liberated. Where you find dictatorships, Islamic domination, Communism, and socialism, women are in bondage. They are considered chattel, nothing more than sex objects or housekeepers. Jesus came to set people free from their bondages!

Paul the Apostle picked up on this concept. "There is neither Jew nor Greek, slave nor free, male nor female, for you are all one in Christ Jesus" (Galatians 3:28). Because of the life, death, and resurrection of Christ Jesus, all distinctions of race, skin color, social status, financial standing, and gender differences are erased. All of us are to be considered on the same level because of Jesus Christ!

In fact, this book could almost be considered a treatise on how Jesus related to women. It shows how he placed a high value on women, lifting them up to be treated as God had planned.

Equality was God's plan from the start. God said, "Let us

make mankind in our image, in our likeness, and let them rule over the fish of the sea and the birds of the air, over the live-stock, over all the earth, and over all the creatures that move along the ground." So God created mankind in his own image, in the image of God he created mankind; male and female he created them! God blessed them and said to them, "Be fruitful and increase in number; fill the earth and subdue it."

Now if you have any doubts as to what God had created and set in motion, look at verse 31, "God saw all that he had made, and it was very good" (Genesis 1:31). For the image of God to be manifested in this world, it took both the male and female. God's original plan was that the two would become one: "For this reason a man will leave his father and mother and be united to his wife, and they will become one flesh" (Genesis 2:24). Why become one? So they will become the complete reflection and image of God.

Then a major problem presented itself. It was only a tree and the fruit of this tree, mixed with the serpent's lies, that changed it all. The plans of God would be thwarted because of sin and separation from God.

There was a promise made that sets the stage for the battle-ground of the ages: God versus Satan, and humans became the battlefield. The war is waged in each person as well as on a global scale. God said, "I will put enmity between you (Satan) and the woman, and between your offspring and hers; he (her offspring, Jesus Christ) will crush your head, and you will strike his heel" (Genesis 3:15). And Satan has been angry with women and waging war against them ever since. Look around and see what's happening in our culture to the woman. Check out her status in the Middle East as well as the Far East.

Jesus came to change and restore what had been stolen from women. He valued them highly. He lifted them up. He treated them as equals. He broke many of the rules in his day by setting them free of the bondages of sin, sickness, and slavery. He came to restore what had been taken and made them forgiven and accepted as equals.

Jesus placed a high value on women. This is one of the best untold secrets and principles of Christianity. Jesus values women! Wherever Christianity has gone, women have been honored with such simple rights as voting, freedom to work, ability to hold property and choose a husband. There are more, but you are catching the idea, I hope.

The world needs this message; the women of this world need to know and believe in this truth. This is one of the most compelling reasons for women to embrace Christianity and its life-changing truths.

Jesus is the liberator of woman who are caught in bondages, distortions, and circumstances of any culture. Something vital is lost to the church when women are not appreciated. Why do we want to set the larger half of our army on the sidelines of life?

Think with me of the barriers Jesus crossed and knocked down in his ministry to women. Note how important they were to his success while here on this earth.

• CONSIDER: God chose a woman, Mary, to give birth to his Son. The Son of God came into this world like all of us through the womb of a woman. Jesus could have come out of the wilderness, fully matured to begin his earthly ministry. Would that have been believable? God chose a woman, a most unlikely one at that—peasant, poor, young, not married—and she came from a "nothing" sort of village, Nazareth.

• CONSIDER: Jesus performed his very first miracle demonstrating his power because of the insistence of a woman, his mother. And it happened at a wedding celebration, of all places. It was a miracle of provision to prolong a party.

- CONSIDER: Jesus told the Samaritan woman at the well the greatest secret in this world: That He, Jesus Christ, is the long-awaited Messiah. She was another unlikely choice. Because the Jews hated the Samaritans, a rabbi or other religious teacher was forbidden to speak to one of them in public, and she was a rank sinner. He overcame and broke down these barriers to help satisfy the spiritually thirsty woman.

- CONSIDER: Mary and Martha, and you remember the details. Understand the culture of that day said that women were not to be taught by a rabbi. Education was reserved only for men and boys. Jesus broke this barrier as he taught Mary and commended her for making the best choice.

- CONSIDER: Who supported him and his band of 12 disciples by providing them with the comforts of home? Food, clothing, shelter, and more, were all freely given from women's own sources. This group of women disciples stayed until Jesus' last breath when he was crucified. Where were his men followers? All, except John, had run into hiding.

- CONSIDER: Jesus never refused to help any woman in need. They came with health issues, financial issues, freedom issues, bondage issues, and more. He helped them and never called a woman a sinner or refused to help because they were not males.

- CONSIDER: Whom did he stop to comfort on his walk up the hill to Golgatha—the women who followed him to the cross. He said, "Don't weep for me, daughters of Jerusalem." They were his most loyal followers.

- CONSIDER: Who were the first at the tomb that Sunday morning? Women! To whom did he make his first personal appearance after his resurrection? A woman! Who was the first real evangelist telling the good news of his resurrection? Read the account, it was the women!

Women are important to the Lord and to his kingdom on

this earth! Women don't give up easily! They have characteristics that will help destroy the kingdoms of this world and build up the kingdom of heaven. They are willing to go in search of needed solutions and answers!

Some of these biblical women we have studied have built their lives on that which is good; others have embraced foolish things and wasted their life. However all of these women have influenced cultures in one way or the other, good or bad. They have been good examples or poor mentors.

Your life and the choices you make are yours. You choose and you reap the good or the bad. But no matter who you are or what you have become, don't give up. There is help, there are answers, there is a solution—his name is Jesus Christ, the King of kings and the Lord of lords. He is a personal Savior for you and your day. He is still the same as he was in the New Testament lives we have looked at, and he will do the same for you!

After these women had their encounter with Jesus, they all left with no more desperation! They left whole. They left with a new purpose in life. They were changed!

And whoever you are, whatever your problem, you may have exhausted all the avenues of help so why not turn to Jesus? The living God is as near as your call for help!

The following is a well-known portrait of Jesus as written by the poet, Myra Welch. Read it carefully; it may be exactly what your desperate soul is craving for.

THIS IS YOUR KING, TOO!

He is a path for the lost.

He is a lamp for the darkness.

He is a robe for the naked.

He is a meal for the hungry.

He is a drink for the thirsty.

He is a source of strength for the weak.

He is a second chance for the fallen.

He is a sight for the blind.

He is a healer for the sick.

He is a treasure for the poor.

He is a reward for the obedient.

He is a joy for the joyless.

He is an open door to the outsider.

He is a shepherd to the sheep.

He is a baptizer to the believer.

He is a friend to the sinner.

He is a companion to the believer.

He is a comforter to the hurting.

He is a lily in the valley.

He is a helper to the helpless.

He is the hope for tomorrow.

He is JESUS!

He is the King of all kings!

He is the Lord of all lords!

He is the fairest of ten thousands and thousands of thousands!

He is from everlasting to everlasting!

He is Alpha and Omega...the Beginning and the End of all things!

He is my Lord and King. He is my personal Savior. He is Supreme!